Formula One MATHS

PRACTICE BOOK

Yvonne Gostling ● Mike Handbury

Bob Hartman ● Howard Johnson

Jean Matthews ● Colin White

C3

SERIES EDITOR: Roger Porkess

HODDER
EDUCATION
PART OF HACHETTE LIVRE UK

Acknowledgements

Every effort has been made to trace and acknowledge ownership of copyright. The publishers will be glad to make suitable arrangements with any copyright holder whom it has not been possible to contact.

Illustrations were drawn by Jeff Edwards and Maggie Brand.

Cover design and page design by Julie Martin.

Hodder Headline's policy is to use papers that are natural, renewable and recyclable products and made from wood grown in sustainable forests. The logging and manufacturing processes conform to the environmental regulations of the country of origin.

Orders: please contact Bookpoint Ltd, 130 Milton Park, Abingdon, Oxon OX14 4SB. Telephone: (44) 01235 827720. Fax (44) 01235 400454. Lines are open from 9.00–5.00, Monday to Saturday, with a 24 hour message answering service. Visit our website at hoddereducation.co.uk.

British Library Cataloguing in Publication Data
A catalogue record for this title is available from The British Library

ISBN: 978 0 340 85930 8

First published 2003
Impression number 10 9 8 7 6 5
Year 2008

Copyright © 2003 Yvonne Gostling, Mike Handbury, Bob Hartman, Howard Johnson, Jean Matthews, Roger Porkess and Colin White

Cover image Jacey, Debut Art

Typeset by Tech-Set Ltd, Gateshead, Tyne & Wear.
Printed in Great Britain for Hodder Education, a part of Hachette Livre UK, 338 Euston Road, London NW1 3BH by Martins the Printers Ltd., Berwick upon Tweed

Contents

1 Percentages

1.1   Financial calculations

1   **(a)**   Copy and complete this table.

50% of 50 goes here.

	50	40	30	5	1
50%	25				
40%		16			
30%			9		
5%					
1%					

(b)   What do you notice about the answers to 30% of 40 and 40% of 30?
What does this imply?

2   Work out the following.

   (a)   50% of £64　　　　**(b)**   10% of 40p　　　　**(c)**   50% of 65 kg

   (d)   64% of £50　　　　**(e)**   40% of 10p　　　　**(f)**   65% of 50 kg

   (g)   75% of £120　　　**(h)**   10% of 15 m　　　**(i)**   15% of 10 m

3   British coins are made from copper, zinc and nickel. This table shows the mass of each coin
and percentage of each metal in £1 and 'silver' coins.

Coin	£1	50p	20p	10p	5p
Mass (g)	9.50	8.00	5.00	6.50	3.25
% copper	70	75	84	75	75
% zinc	24.5	0	0	0	0
% nickel	5.5	25	16	25	25

   (a)   What is the mass of nickel in each of these coins?

      (i)   50p　　　　　　　**(ii)**   20p　　　　　　　**(iii)** £1

   (b)   Which coin contains the highest proportion of copper?

   (c)   What coin contains the greatest mass of copper?

   (d)   What mass of nickel is there in £10 worth of 20p coins?

4   Find six pairs of numbers that make this statement true.

$$\underline{\hspace{2cm}}\% \text{ of } \underline{\hspace{2cm}} = 20$$

Be adventurous, use some 'difficult' numbers!

5   Which is the better offer 30% off or $\frac{1}{3}$ off?
Explain how you worked out your answer.

1.2   Profit and loss

To calculate the percentage change in N you use the formula $\dfrac{\text{Change in } N}{\text{Original value of } N} \times 100\%.$

In this exercise give your answers to 2 decimal places where necessary.

1 The cost price of a DVD player is £20.
   (a) It is priced at £35. What is the percentage profit?
   (b) A profit of 45% is made. What is the selling price?

2 **(a)** The cost price of a dress is £40. It is sold for a profit of 12.5%.
         What is the selling price?
   (b) The cost price of a pair of trousers is £56. They are sold for £58.24.
         What is the percentage profit?
   (c) The cost price of a coat is £124. It is sold at a loss of 7%.
         What is the selling price?

3 Amy is an antique dealer.
   (a) She buys a table for £600. She sells the table for £750.
         What is her percentage profit?
   (b) **(i)** She buys another table for £1450. She prices it to make a profit of 15%.
              What is the selling price?
        (ii) She sells the table for only £1232.50.
              What is her percentage loss?

4 This table shows the populations, in millions, of London and Paris from 1980 to 2020.

	Year			
	1980	1990	2000	2020*
Paris	9.01	9.33	9.63	9.89
London	8.06	7.84	7.63	7.63

*estimated population

   (a) Find the percentage change in the population of Paris from
        (i) 1980 to 1990
        (ii) 1990 to 2000
        (iii) 2000 to 2020.
   (b) Find the percentage change in the population of London from
        (i) 1980 to 1990
        (ii) 1990 to 2000
        (iii) 2000 to 2020.

5   The table shows the number of hectares, in millions, that are used for growing rice in Asia and the rest of the world in 1961 and 2001.

	Asia	Rest of world
1961	107	8
2001	139	15

(a)   What was the total area, in millions of hectares, used to grow rice in 1961?

(b)   What percentage, to the nearest 1%, of the total in 1961 was in Asia?

(c)   What was the percentage change in the area used to produce rice in Asia from 1961 to 2001.

(d)   What was the change for the rest of the world?

6   **Investigation**

It is possible to have an increase of 100%. What does it mean?
What about a decrease of 100%?

1.3   Reverse percentage calculations

1 Find the numbers given by these clues.
  (a) One-third of the number is 12.   (b) Two-thirds of the number is 18.
  (c) Three-quarters of the number is 48.   (d) 50% of the number is 11.
  (e) 20% of the number is 15.   (f) 150% of the number is 15.

2 All items in a sports shop are reduced by 10% in a sale.
  Find the original prices of items with these prices in the sale.
  (a) £18   (b) £72   (c) £180   (d) £117

3 As a result of rising fuel costs a tour operator increases the price of its holidays by 5%.
  What were the original prices of holidays now costing these amounts?
  Give your answers to the nearest penny.
  (a) £200   (b) £262   (c) £525   (d) £300

4 This rule gives the original price of an object reduced by 20% in a sale.
  Multiply the sale price by five and divide the answer by four.
  (a) Use the rule to find the original prices of items in the sale costing these amounts.
      (i)   £24   (ii) £72   (iii) £22   (iv) £66
  (b) Find a similar rule which works for sale reductions of   (i) 60%   (ii) 5%.
      Hint: You might find it useful to set up and solve an equation.

5 This table shows the protein, fat and water content of various cheeses.

Cheese	% Protein	% Fat	% Water
Edam	24	23	53
Processed	22	25	53
Parmesan	35	30	35
Stilton	26	40	34

James likes cheese but is only allowed 10 g of fat in any cheese he eats.
Find, to the nearest gram, how much he is allowed to eat of each type of cheese.

6 The fruit machines in Las Vegas pay out about 95% of the money that is put into them.
  (a) Over one week a fruit machine has $200 000 put into it.
      About how much money does the casino take?
  (b) About how much money would you need to put in to be fairly sure of receiving $500 in
      prize money?

7 For an average bungee jumper bungee cord stretches by 90% at the end of a jump.
  (a) What length will a 10 m bungee cord be at the end of a jump?
  (b) Amy is about average weight. She wants to bungee jump from a bridge 38 m high.
      What length of bungee cord should she use?

1.4   Interest

You will need to use the following formulae in this exercise.

$$I = \frac{PRT}{100} \text{ and } A = P\left(1 + \frac{R}{100}\right)^T$$

The first is used to calculate simple interest. The second is used to calculate the amount payable on an investment earning compound interest.

£P is the money invested, £I is the interest earned, $R\%$ per year is the interest rate, T is the time invested, in years, and £A is the total amount due.

1   Use your calculator to work out the values of these expressions.
Give your answers correct to 2 decimal places.
    (a) $\dfrac{150 \times 76 \times 0.25}{100}$ **(b)** $\dfrac{14 \times 24 \times 0.5}{100}$ **(c)** $60\left(1 + \dfrac{7}{100}\right)^5$ **(d)** $750\left(1 + \dfrac{11}{100}\right)^3$

2   Write down a formula to give the amount, A, payable on an investment earning simple interest.
State what each letter in your formula represents.

3   Find the simple interest payable and the total amount payable on the following.
    (a) £250 invested for 6 years at 7% p.a.
    (b) £650 invested for 4 years at 4% p.a.
    (c) £200 invested for 8 years at 4.5% p.a.
    (d) £360 invested for 3 years at 6% p.a.

4   Find the total amount payable, to the nearest penny, with compound interest on the following.
    (a) £250 invested for 6 years at 7% p.a.
    (b) £650 invested for 4 years at 4% p.a.
    (c) £200 invested for 8 years at 4.5% p.a.
    (d) £360 invested for 3 years at 6% p.a.

5   **(a)** What is the total amount due, to the nearest penny, on £1 invested for 100 years at a rate of 5% compound interest?
    (b) What is the total amount due when 5% simple interest is paid on the investment in **(a)**?

6   Every year a computer loses about 30% of its value at the start of that year.
The original cost of a computer is £1300. How much is it worth, to the nearest penny, after
    (a) 1 year   **(b)** 2 years   **(c)** 3 years?

7   Human populations grow like money invested with compound interest.
Surat is a large city in India. Its population in 2000 was 2.7 million.
Its population is growing at the rate of 5% per year.
What is its expected population, in millions, in 2010?
Give your answer to 2 decimal places.

8   Which of these investments gives the greater sum?
    (a) £100 invested at compound interest of 5% for 25 years.
    (b) £100 invested at simple interest of 13% for 25 years.

2 Algebraic expressions

2.1 Review

1 Simplify these expressions.
(a) $2x + 5 + 7x - 3x + 6$
(b) $4 - 6y + y - 2 + 7 + 9y$
(c) $4a + 5b + 7a + 2b - a$
(d) $3c + 4d + 7d + 2d - 5c + 2c$

2 Group together the algebra cards with matching expressions.

$3y$	$y^2 + y^2 + y^2$	3 less than y	$y \times 3$
$5y - 2y$	$y - 3$	$y + y + y$	$3 \times y^2$
$3 + y$	$-(3 - y)$	3 lots of y^2	3 more than y
$3y \times y$			$1 + y + 2$

3 Find the value of $b(a + c)$ when
(a) $a = 3, b = 4, c = 2$
(b) $a = 3, b = 4, c = -3$
(c) $a = 0, b = 3, c = 2$
(d) $a = 7, b = 0, c = -2$.

4 Expand these brackets.
(a) $5(3 + 2s)$ (b) $4(3 - 5t)$ (c) $3(4v - 7)$ (d) $-2(3w - 5)$

5 Factorise these expressions fully.
(a) $6 - 9p$ (b) $15 + 10q$ (c) $16x + 20y$ (d) $35x - 42y$

6 Expand and simplify these expressions.
(a) $5(3a + 1) + 4(2a + 3)$
(b) $6(5b - 4) + 2(b + 6)$
(c) $6(2c + 5) - 3(c + 4)$
(d) $2(5d + 3) - 4(d - 1)$
(e) $3(8e - 5) + 5(e - 6)$
(f) $f + 9 - 6(2f - 6)$
(g) $4(g + 3) - (g - 1)$
(h) $5(2h - 3) - 2(3 - h)$

2.2 Indices

1 Write each of the following as a single power.

(a) $a^4 \times a^3$ (b) $b^2 \times b^5$ (c) $c^8 \times c^{20}$ (d) $d \times d^3$

(e) $e^6 \div e$ (f) $f^7 \div f^3$ (g) $g^{20} \div g^{20}$ (h) $h^{35} \div h^{34}$

2 Meena simplifies $3y^2 \times 4y^4$ like this.

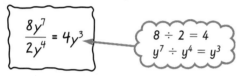

$$3y^2 \times 4y^4 = 3 \times 4 \times y^2 \times y^4$$
$$= 12y^6$$

Simplify the following.

(a) $5a^3 \times 2a^2$ (b) $6b^8 \times 5b^3$ (c) $4c^{15} \times 12c^5$ (d) $9d^{199} \times 2d$

3 Meena simplifies $\dfrac{8y^7}{2y^4}$ like this.

$$\frac{8y^7}{2y^4} = 4y^3$$

$8 \div 2 = 4$
$y^7 \div y^4 = y^3$

Simplify the following.

(a) $\dfrac{12a^6}{3a^2}$ (b) $\dfrac{30b^{10}}{5b^2}$ (c) $\dfrac{100c^{100}}{20c^{20}}$ (d) $\dfrac{25d^6}{5d^3}$

4 $2^3 \div 2^3 = 2^0$ and $2^3 \div 2^3 = 8 \div 8 = 1$

Give three more examples like this to demonstrate that $n^0 = 1$ for any value of n.

5 Write each of the following as a single power.

(a) $(p^2)^5$ (b) $(q^3)^4$ (c) $(r^8)^{10}$ (d) $(s^{50})^6$

6 Abigail simplifies $(2y^3)^4$ like this.

$$(2y^3)^4 = 2y^3 \times 2y^3 \times 2y^3 \times 2y^3$$
$$= 2^4 y^{12}$$
$$= 16y^{12}$$

Simplify the following.

(a) $(3t^3)^2$ (b) $(2u^4)^3$ (c) $(5v^6)^2$ (d) $(2w^7)^5$

2.3   Expanding two brackets

① Expand the following brackets.
- **(a)** $a(4a + 3)$
- **(b)** $b(5b - 2)$
- **(c)** $2c(c + 5)$
- **(d)** $3d(2d - 7)$
- **(e)** $e(3 + e^2)$
- **(f)** $5f(2f^2 - 7)$
- **(g)** $g(1 + 2g + 3g^2)$
- **(h)** $5h(2 - 3h + h^2)$
- **(i)** $6i(3i^2 - 2i + 4)$

② Factorise these expressions fully.
- **(a)** $a^2 + 6a$
- **(b)** $4b^2 + 8b$
- **(c)** $12c^2 - 8c$
- **(d)** $d^3 - 9d^2$
- **(e)** $e^3 + 5e^2 - 8e$
- **(f)** $6f^3 + 12f^2 + 3f$

③ Expand the following brackets. Simplify your answers.
- **(a)** $(a + 4)(a + 2)$
- **(b)** $(b + 5)(b + 1)$
- **(c)** $(c - 1)(c + 7)$
- **(d)** $(d + 4)(d - 3)$
- **(e)** $(e - 2)(e - 5)$
- **(f)** $(f - 4)(f - 3)$

④
- **(a)** **(i)** Expand and simplify $(x + 6)^2$.
  - **(ii)** Substitute $x = 10$ in your answer to **(i)** and find the value of your expression.
- **(b)** **(i)** Expand and simplify $(x - 4)^2$.
  - **(ii)** Substitute $x = 20$ in your answer to **(i)** and find the value of your expression.
- **(c)** Your answers to **(a)(ii)** and **(b)(ii)** should be the same.
  Look at the original expressions you were asked to expand and explain why the results are the same.

⑤ Expand and simplify the following.
- **(a)** $(m + 4)^2$
- **(b)** $(n - 5)^2$
- **(c)** $(p + 6)^2$
- **(d)** $(q - 7)^2$

⑥ Expand and simplify the following.
- **(a)** $(r + 3)(r - 3)$
- **(b)** $(s + 7)(s - 7)$
- **(c)** $(t - 5)(t + 5)$
- **(d)** $(u - 8)(u + 8)$

2.4   Further expressions

1   Simplify the following.
   (a) $2a^2 + 5a + 13a + 6a^2$
   (b) $6b^3 + 9b + 5b^3 - 4b$
   (c) $5c^2 + 2bc + 8c^2 - 3bc$
   (d) $2d^3 + 8c^2d + d^3 + 2c^2d$
   (e) $e^3 + 3e^2 - 2e + 5e^3 - 7e$
   (f) $6ef - 9e^2f - 2ef + 3e^2f$

2   Simplify the following.
   (a) $8a^3b \times 2ab^2$
   (b) $3c^2d^2 \times 4c^3d^4$
   (c) $5e^6f^2 \times 4e^4f$
   (d) $9gh^8 \times 3gh^4$
   (e) $4xy^5 \times 25x^4y^{10}$
   (f) $2k^6m^2 \times 6k^3m^2n \times 5kn^3$

3   Simplify the following.
   (a) $\dfrac{12a^6b^3}{3a^2b}$
   (b) $\dfrac{15c^8d^5}{5c^3d^2}$
   (c) $\dfrac{80e^{10}f^6g^8}{20e^5f^4}$
   (d) $\dfrac{35x^6y^{20}}{5x^3y^{12}}$
   (e) $\dfrac{15x^8y^5z^{19}}{3x^3y^4z^9}$
   (f) $\dfrac{100m^{10}n^{60}p^{25}}{5m^8n^{42}p^{17}}$

4   (a)   Show that the surface area, S cm², of this cuboid is given by
              $S = 2x(x + 2h)$.
      (b)   Find the surface area when $x = 5$ and $h = 20$.

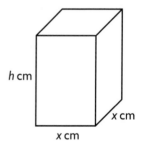

h cm

x cm

x cm

5   Factorise these expressions fully.
   (a) $6ab + 9a$
   (b) $12cd - 6c^2$
   (c) $8e^2f + 8e^2$
   (d) $10gh - 20g^2$
   (e) $5jk^2 + 10jk$
   (f) $100m^2n - 1000mn$

3 Doing a survey

3.1 Collecting information

1 Explain what is wrong with each of these survey questions.
   (a) Does your family watch a lot of television?
   (b) Fox hunting should be banned. Do you agree?

   yes ☐   no ☐

   (c) How old are you?

   Over 30 ☐   Under 21 ☐   Under 16 ☐

   (d) How interesting do you think maths is?

   very interesting ☐   interesting ☐   quite interesting ☐

   (e) When they are not playing at home, United are not a good side at scoring goals. Do you disagree?

2 **(a)** Design a questionnaire to find out what people have for their breakfast.
   (b) Design a questionnaire to find out if boys have more pocket money than girls.

3 Explain what is wrong with the method used in each of these surveys. Give at least two reasons.
   (a) A newspaper carried out a survey to find out which party the majority of people would vote for in an election.
   They chose names from the telephone directory and phoned the number.
   (b) Students at a school think they are given too much homework.
   To gauge opinion they ask students coming out of the dining hall at lunchtime.
   (c) The manager of a new pop group wants to know if their new release will be popular.
   She goes into the local library on Friday between 12 noon and 1 pm and asks people their opinion.

4 Five people are asked to taste three new varieties of crisps. They rate the varieties 1 (best), 2 or 3 (worst). Here are the results.

	Person				
Flavour	A	B	C	D	E
Curry	1	3	3	1	3
Pizza	3	2	1	3	1
Sweet 'n' sour	2	1	2	2	2

How would you decide which is the most popular new flavour?
Suggest more than one method.

3.2   Displaying data

You will need squared paper for this exercise.

1   Elizabeth asks the students in her class what pets they have. Here are her results.

Budgie (B)		Cat (C)		Dog (D)		Fish (F)		Rabbit (R)	
C	F	B	B	D	F	F	R	C	R
C	D	F	B	R	C	B	R	R	B
R	D	D	R	C	C	D	D	C	C

(a)   Make a tally chart to show these results.
(b)   What can you say about the number of students in the class?
(c)   What is the most popular pet in the class?
(d)   Draw a bar chart to show these results.

2   This multiple bar chart gives the number of boys and girls in each year of a secondary school.

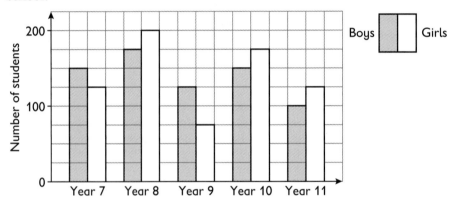

(a)   In which years are there more boys than girls?
(b)   How many boys and how many girls are there in the school altogether?
(c)   On average, each Year 11 student takes eight GCSE exams.
       What is the total number of exam entries in Year 11?

3   The ages of people in one village, one town and one city are recorded.
They are summarised in the table below.

Age	Village	Town	City
Under 15	25%	25%	20%
15 to 60	35%	55%	70%
Over 60	40%	20%	10%

(a)   Draw a compound bar chart to illustrate these data.
(b)   Compare the age distributions in the village, the town and the city.

3.3   Pie charts

You will need a protractor and a pair of compasses for this exercise.

1   Year 9 students in a school have 40 lessons each week.
The table shows how the lessons are divided between the subjects.

Maths	English	Science	Technology	Humanities	Others
5	5	6	4	8	12

  (a)   How many degrees are needed to represent one lesson?
  (b)   Draw a pie chart to show the data.
  (c)   (i)   What percentage of the lessons is on humanities and others together?
       (ii)   What percentage of the lessons is on maths and English together?

2   This pie chart illustrates the first 200 vehicles to pass through a village one morning.

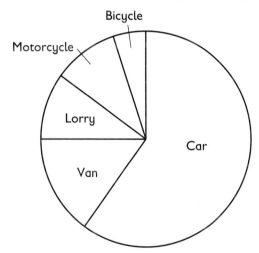

Copy and complete the following table to find the numbers of each type of vehicle.

Vehicle type	Angle	Fraction	Number of vehicles
Van	54°	$\frac{54}{360}$	$\frac{54}{360} \times 200 = 30$
Lorry			
Motorcycle			
Bicycle			
Car			

3   (a)   Make a table like the one in question 1 to show how the lessons in your school week
       are divided between the subjects.
  (b)   Draw a pie chart to illustrate the data.
  (c)   What are the differences and similarities between your pie chart and that in question 1?

3.4   Working with grouped data

You will need squared paper for this exercise.

1   Each student in a class of 30 is weighed. Here are the weights, in kilograms.

51.9	52.9	53.4	65.2	55.8	63.5	56.1	60.3	57.2	59.4
51.4	54.8	55.9	55.3	56.2	65.5	57.0	57.6	58.1	58.7
58.7	58.8	59.2	60.1	61.3	61.8	62.3	63.1	64.1	59.4

(a)   Copy and complete this table.

Weight (w kg)	$50 < w \leqslant 54$	$54 < w \leqslant 58$	$58 < w \leqslant 62$	$62 < w \leqslant 66$
Tally				
Frequency				

(b)   Is weight a discrete or a continuous variable?
(c)   Which is the modal group of the data?
(d)   Draw a frequency chart to illustrate the data.

2   A policeman records the speeds of cars driving
through a village. He displays the data he collects
on Sunday as a frequency polygon.
(a)   Is speed a discrete or a continuous variable?
(b)   How many cars are there in Sunday's survey?
(c)   What does the diagram tell you?

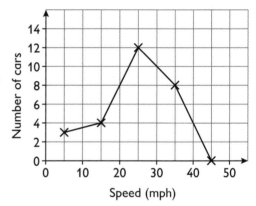

Here are Monday's data.

31.2	23.5	7.2	29.4	36.3	42.8	31.7
35.4	27.2	30.3	9.5	48.6	26.6	38.8
15.9	22.3	31.1	37.4	39.8	47.0	32.1
38.0	30.2	20.7	35.0	38.1		

(d)   Copy and complete this frequency table for the data.

Speed (v mph)	$0 < v \leqslant 10$	$10 < v \leqslant 20$	$20 < v \leqslant 30$	$30 < v \leqslant 40$	$40 < v \leqslant 50$
Tally					
Frequency					

(e)   The speed limit through the village is 40 mph.
      How many cars exceeded the speed limit?
(f)   How many of the cars do you think had just set off or were just stopping?
(g)   (i)   Copy the frequency polygon for Sunday's data.
      (ii)   Add a frequency polygon for Monday's data to your diagram.
(h)   Compare the speeds on the two days.

3   Make a list of
(a)   five discrete numerical variables
(b)   five continuous numerical variables
(c)   five categorical variables.

3.5   Scatter diagrams

You will need graph paper for this exercise.

1 (a) Copy and complete these statements.
   (i) Positive correlation means 'As one variable increases, the other _____'.
   (ii) Negative correlation means 'As one variable increases, the other _____'.

(b) Do you think there will be positive, negative or no correlation between each of these pairs of variables?
   (i) The number of flowers and the number of bees in a garden.
   (ii) The number of cars on the road and the number of road accidents.
   (iii) The number of policemen patrolling the streets and the number of burglaries.
   (iv) The number of televisions bought and the number of passengers on public transport.
   (v) The mileage which a car has done and the depth of tread on its tyres.

2 Students leaving a maths exam are asked what size of shoe they wear. The exam mark and shoe size of each student are recorded in this scatter diagram.

(a) What are the highest and lowest exam marks?

(b) What are the largest and smallest shoe sizes?

(c) What is the most popular shoe size?

(d) Paul wears size 6 shoes. What is his exam mark?

(e) Describe the correlation.

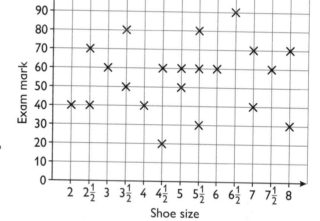

3 The engine size and fuel consumption of fourteen cars are given in the table.

(a) Draw a scatter diagram to illustrate these data.

(b) Draw a line of best fit on your diagram.

(c) Use the line of best fit to estimate
   (i) the engine size of a car which has a fuel consumption of 30 mpg.
   (ii) the fuel consumption of a car which has an engine size of 1600 cc.

Engine size (cc)	Fuel consumption (mpg)
2000	40
1000	50
1500	40
2000	35
900	55
3000	25
1000	45
2500	35
3200	20
2400	28
3500	20
1300	36
1300	42
2000	28

4 Equations

4.1 Solving equations

In this exercise set out your working step by step.

1 Solve these equations and check your answers.
- **(a)** $3x - 2 = 4$
- **(b)** $2x + 7 = 12$
- **(c)** $6x + 2 = 3x + 5$
- **(d)** $5x - 1 = 4x + 3$
- **(e)** $x + 7 = 5$
- **(f)** $2x + 4 = 4x + 1$
- **(g)** $5(x - 3) = 6x$
- **(h)** $2(x + 7) - 1 = 9$
- **(i)** $4(2x + 3) - 3(x + 4) = 0$
- **(j)** $6(x - 3) + 5(2x - 7) = 2(3x + 2)$

2 Solve these equations and check your answers.
- **(a)** $\dfrac{a}{3} = 7$
- **(b)** $\dfrac{b - 3}{5} = 6$
- **(c)** $\dfrac{c}{4} = 24$
- **(d)** $\dfrac{d + 1}{6} = \dfrac{1}{3}$
- **(e)** $\dfrac{5}{e} = \dfrac{2}{5}$
- **(f)** $\dfrac{2f}{5} - 4 = 3$
- **(g)** $\frac{1}{2}(g - 3) = \frac{1}{3}(g + 2)$
- **(h)** $\dfrac{h + 1}{7} = \dfrac{h - 4}{2}$
- **(i)** $\frac{1}{5}(2x + 3) + \frac{1}{4}(3x - 2) = 7$
- **(j)** $\frac{3}{4}(y + 8) = 7 + \frac{1}{3}(y + 2)$

3 Alan and Ruth are making up number puzzles for each other.

I think of a number.
I multiply it by 4 then add 3.
My answer is twice the
number I thought of.

I think of a number.
I add 5 and halve the result.
The answer is 31.

Alan

Ruth

Write equations and solve them to find the numbers that Alan and Ruth were thinking of.

4 Solve these equations.

- **(a)** $3a - 1\frac{1}{2} = 2a + 5\frac{1}{4}$
- **(b)** $\dfrac{b - 2}{5} = \dfrac{b + 7}{3}$
- **(c)** $6.3c + 4.1 = 5.6c + 6.9$
- **(d)** $5d - 4.8 = 4.2d + 9.2$
- **(e)** $\frac{1}{2}(4g - 3) = 5g - 7$
- **(f)** $\dfrac{3h + 1}{5} = \dfrac{1}{2}(h - 3)$
- **(g)** $\frac{1}{4}(2x + 5) + 1 = \frac{3}{4}(x - 2)$
- **(h)** $0.6y + 5.2 = \frac{1}{3}(6.3y + 2.1)$

4.2   Solving more equations

1   To solve the equation $12 - 5x = 2$, one possible first step is to add $5x$ to both sides.
Use a similar method to solve these equations.

(a) $16 - 3a = 7$

(b) $20 - 6b = 5$

(c) $11 = 19 - 4c$

(d) $5 - 2d = 2$

(e) $12 = 18 - 5e$

(f) $6 = 8.5 - 5f$

(g) $9.2 - 3g = 7.4$

(h) $5 - \frac{1}{2}h = 1$

(i) $18 - 5x = 0$

2   To solve the equation $12 - 5x = 2$, another possible first step is to subtract 12 from both sides and then divide both sides by -5.
Use a similar method to solve these equations.

(a) $8 - 3a = 5$

(b) $12 - 7b = -2$

(c) $1 - 5c = 31$

(d) $16 = 18 - 10d$

(e) $5 = 40 - 7e$

(f) $8 - 1.2f = 20$

(g) $4 - \frac{1}{2}g = 13$

(h) $6.1 - 1.3h = 10$

(i) $10 - 1.5x = 13$

3   Solve these equations. Check by substitution that your answers are correct.

(a) $6 - 5x = 4$

(b) $6(2 - x) = 18$

(c) $\frac{1}{5}(x - 3) = 4$

(d) $\frac{1}{4}(3 - 2x) = 6$

(e) $6(x + 2) - 5(2x + 1) = 14$

(f) $8(4 - x) = 6(1 - 2x)$

(g) $6.8 - 3.5x = 4.7$

(h) $\dfrac{7 - 2x}{5} = \dfrac{4 - x}{3}$

(i) $2.5x + 8 = 0$

(j) $7(3x - 2) + 5(1 - x) = 0$

4.3   Forming equations

1   Look at this rectangle.
  (a)   What does x represent on the diagram?
  (b)   Write an expression in terms of x for the perimeter of
        the rectangle. Simplify your expression.
  (c)   The perimeter is 48 cm.
        Write and solve an equation to find x.
  (d)   What are the dimensions of the rectangle?

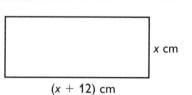

x cm

$(x + 12)$ cm

2   Jane's age now is n years.
  (a)   Write down an expression for her age in 4 years' time.
  (b)   Write down an expression for her age 7 years ago.

In 4 years' time
I will be twice as old as I
was 7 years ago.
How old am I now?

  (c)   Write an equation and solve it to find n.

3   The cost of hiring a car from Charlie's Cars is £15 a day plus 5p a mile.
  (a)   Work out the cost for one day when 340 miles are travelled.
  (b)   Write down an expression for the hire cost for one day when n miles are travelled.
  (c)   Write an equation and solve it to find the number of miles travelled when the hire
        cost is £26.

4   **Activity** ───

  Make up your own 'Think of a number' puzzle and write it down.
  Keep the answer separate.
  Swap your puzzle with a friend.
  Form and solve an equation to find the answer to your friend's puzzle.
  Check with your friend that you got the correct answer.

4.4   Trial and improvement

1 Copy and complete the table to solve this equation.

$$x^3 - x = 20$$

Give your answer correct to 1 decimal place.

x	x^3	$x^3 - x$	small/large

2 Make your own table to solve this equation.

$$x^3 + 2x = 50$$

Give your answer correct to 2 decimal places.

3 Sumita uses a spreadsheet to solve this equation.

$$x^3 - 10x = 2$$

She enters possible values of x in column A then enters a formula in cell B2 and copies the formula down column B.

	A	B
1	x	$x^3 - 10x$
2	3	

(a) What formula should she enter in cell B2?

(b) Use a spreadsheet or table to find one root of the equation, correct to 2 decimal places.

(c) There are three roots altogether. Find the other two, giving your answers correct to 2 decimal places.

4 Sam has a piece of card 20 cm by 30 cm.
He cuts a square of side x cm out of each corner and folds up the rest to make a tray.
Copy and complete the table of values to find the value of x which gives the largest volume for the tray.
Give your answer correct to 2 decimal places.

20 cm

30 cm

x	Volume (cm³)
2	$16 \times 26 \times 2 =$
3	

5 Make tables or use a spreadsheet to solve these equations.
Give your answers correct to 2 decimal places.

(a) $x^3 + 5x = 55$

(b) $x^3 - x^2 = 80$

5 Working with polygons

5.1 Angles

1 Calculate the size of each lettered angle in these shapes.

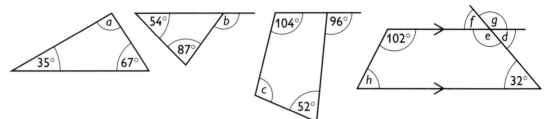

2 ABCDE is a pentagon.
  (a) Calculate the size of the following angles.
    (i) $A\hat{B}E$
    (ii) $E\hat{B}C$
    (iii) $C\hat{D}E$
  (b) What is the sum of all the interior angles of this pentagon?

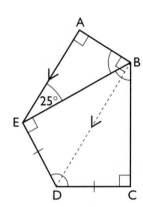

3 This pentagon is made up of three isosceles triangles.
  (a) Calculate the size of all the lettered angles.
  (b) What is the sum of the interior angles of this pentagon?

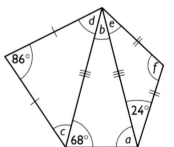

4 The angles on a straight line add up to 180°.
The interior angles of a quadrilateral add up to 360°.
Use these facts to prove that the exterior angles of a quadrilateral,
$A + B + C + D$, add up to 360°.

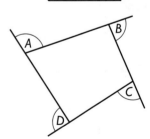

5 A boat B is on a bearing of 046° from a lighthouse L and
317° from the coastguard station C.
  (a) What is the bearing of
    (i) the lighthouse from the boat
    (ii) the coastguard station from the boat?
  (b) Calculate angle LBC.

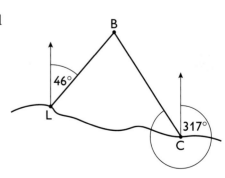

5.2 Angles of polygons

1 (a) This octagon has been split into triangles.
Show how you use the sum of angles in a triangle to calculate
the sum of the interior angles of an octagon.

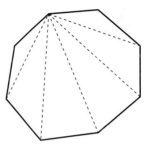

(b) This diagram shows a square inside a regular octagon.
Show how you use the sum of the angles in a quadrilateral
and the sum of the angles in a triangle to calculate the sum
of the angles in an octagon.

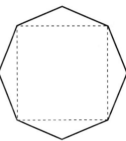

2 Calculate the sum of the interior angles of
  (a) a pentagon   (b) a decagon
  (c) a enneagon   (d) a polygon with 20 sides.

3 Calculate the interior angle of
  (a) a regular dodecagon (12 sides)
  (b) a regular polygon with 15 sides.

4 The sum of the interior angles of a polygon is 2520°.
How many sides does it have?

5 Angela says 'all quadrilaterals tessellate'.
Is she correct?
Draw a diagram to show whether or not she is correct.

6 (a) The formula for the sum of the angles in an n-sided polygon is
$$S = (n - 2) \times 180.$$
Write down the formula for i, the interior angle of a regular n-sided polygon.

  (b) Show that your formula is the same as
$$i = \frac{(2n - 4) \times 90}{n}.$$

7 (a) Calculate i, the interior angle of a regular n-sided polygon, when
    (i) $n = 18$ (ii) $n = 180$ (iii) $n = 360$ (iv) $n = 720$.
  (b) What do you notice about your answers to **(a)**?

5.3   Regular polygons

You will need a protractor and a pair of compasses for this exercise.

1 A regular polygon has an exterior angle of 20°.
   (a) What is the sum of the exterior angles?
   (b) How many sides does the polygon have?
   (c) What is the size of each interior angle?
   (d) What is the sum of the interior angles?

2 **(a)** Calculate the exterior angle of a regular dodecagon (12 sides).
   (b) Make an accurate construction of a dodecagon.
   (c) What is the interior angle of a regular dodecagon?

3 Gemma is drawing a regular polygon.
This is the start of her diagram.
   (a) How many sides does the polygon have?
   (b) What is the exterior angle of the polygon?
   (c) What is the interior angle of the polygon?

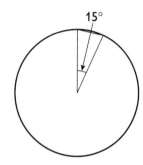

4 A regular polygon has an exterior angle of 12°.
   (a) Calculate the interior angle.
   (b) How many sides does the polygon have?

5 The interior angle of a regular polygon is 170°.
   (a) Calculate the exterior angle of the polygon.
   (b) How many sides does the polygon have?

6 Calculate
   (i) the exterior angle   **(ii)** the number of sides
of regular polygons with the following interior angles.
   (a) 144°   **(b)** 156°   **(c)** 171°   **(d)** 172°

7 Show that the exterior angle of a regular polygon cannot be 25°.

8 The interior angle of an n-sided regular polygon can be calculated using the formula
$180 - \dfrac{360}{n}$.
Show this gives the same result as $\dfrac{(n-2) \times 180}{n}$.

9 A robot is programmed to start from A and travel in a
clockwise direction back to A.
   (a) Copy and complete these instructions

     Forward 20, right 60°
     Forward 30, right …

   (b) The robot turns through six angles altogether.
      What is the sum of these angles?

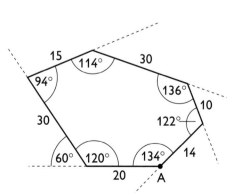

5.4   Pythagoras' rule

In this exercise give your answers correct to 1 decimal place where necessary.

1   Copy and complete this calculation to find c.

$c^2 = 4.5^2 + 6^2$
$c^2 = 20.25 + 36$
$c^2 = \square$
$c = \square$

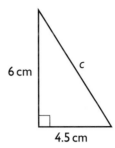

2   Find the length of the hypotenuse of each of these triangles.

(a)

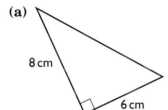

(b)

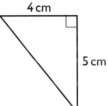

(c)

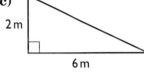

3   This is a plan of Felicity's lawn.
There is a path from corner to corner.
How long is the path?

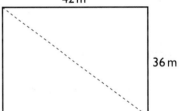

4   Calculate the perimeters of these shapes.

(a)

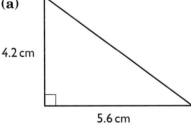

(b)

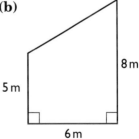

5   The diameter of the glass is 6 cm. The height of the glass is 9 cm.
What is the length of a straw that stands in the glass with 1 cm of
straw outside the glass?

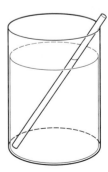

5.5 Using Pythagoras' rule

In this exercise give your answers correct to 1 decimal place where necessary.

1 Find the lengths of the sides marked with a letter in each of these triangles.

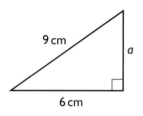
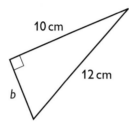
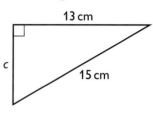

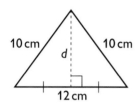
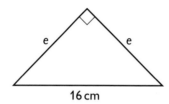
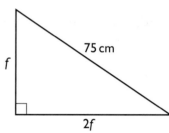

2 Jeff is using a rubbish skip.
He puts a plank against the skip
to make a ramp.
The plank is 2 m long and
overhangs the skip by 15 cm.
How far is the bottom of the
plank from the edge of the
skip?

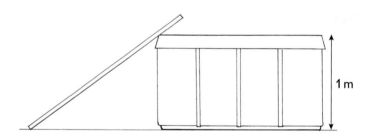

3 The diagram shows the frame of a children's slide.
   (a) Calculate the length of the ladder, l.
   (b) Calculate the height of the slide, h.

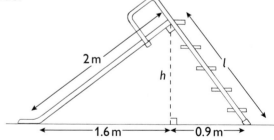

4 **Investigation**

A paint stirrer is 19 cm long.
When it stands in the can there must be at least 2 cm but
not more than 4 cm extending over the edge of the can.
The diameter and height of the paint can are whole number
values and the diameter is at least 8 cm.
   (a) Find all the possible values of the diameter and height
      of the paint can.
   (b) How many of your results are Pythagorean triples?

6 Sequences and functions

6.1 Generating sequences

1 Find the first five terms of the following sequences.
(a) $n \rightarrow 3n$
(b) The first term is 5. To find the next term, double the previous term.
(c) $T(n) = n^2 + 1$
(d) $n \rightarrow 20 - 5n$

2 Match these sequences with their functions.
(a) $2, 4, 6, 8, \ldots$ (i) $t_n = 2^n$
(b) $0, 4, 8, 12, \ldots$ (ii) $n \rightarrow n^2$
(c) $1, 4, 9, 16, \ldots$ (iii) $T(n) = 2n$
(d) $2, 4, 8, 16, \ldots$ (iv) The first term is 1. To find the next term add 3 to the previous term.
(e) $1, 4, 7, 10, \ldots$ (v) $n \rightarrow 4(n - 1)$

3 A sequence is given by $T(n) = 5n - 2$.
(a) Find the 100th term of the sequence.
(b) Write down the first four terms of the sequence.
(c) Find the term-to-term rule for this sequence.

4 Each of these numbers is in just one of the sequences (a) to (f).
Find which sequence each number is in.

     81   48   50   −5   −9   157

(a) $n \rightarrow 20 - 5n$
(b) The first term is 6. To find the next term double the previous term.
(c) $n \rightarrow 2n^2$
(d) $T(n) = 5n + 2$
(e) $t_n = 3^n$
(f) The first term is zero. To find the next term subtract 3 from the previous term.

6.2   Linear patterns

1   Which of these sequences are linear?
   (a)   1, 4, 7, 10, 13, ...   **(b)**   1, 1, 2, 3, 5, ...   **(c)**   1, 2, 4, 8, 16, ...
   (d)   10, 6, 2, −2, −6, ...   **(e)**   25, 28, 31, 34, 37, ...   **(f)**   2, 5, 10, 17, 26, ...

2   Jenny collects teddy bears.
   She was given three when she was born and gets two more for her birthday each year.
   (a)   How many teddy bears does she have when she is 14?
   (b)   Write a formula to show how many she will have when her age is n years.

3   For each of these sequences, find
   (i)   the formula for the nth term   **(ii)**   the 150th term.
   (a)   6, 10, 14, 18, ...   **(b)**   45, 50, 55, 60, ...   **(c)**   99, 98, 97, 96, ...
   (d)   24, 21, 18, 15, ...   **(e)**   20, 21.5, 23, 24.5, ...   **(f)**   18, 11, 4, −3, ...

4   A formula for a sequence is $T(n) = 3n + 7$.
   (a)   Write down the first five terms of the sequence.
   (b)   How does the '3' in the formula affect the sequence?
   (c)   Explain where the '7' in the formula comes from.
   (d)   Which term in the sequence has the value 70?

5   Peter has £20 in his savings account. He gets a paper round and decides to put £4 each
   week into his account.
   (a)   How much will be in his account after
       (i)   2 weeks   **(ii)**   12 weeks   **(iii)** n weeks?
   (b)   How long after he starts his paper round is it before he has £100 in his account?

6.3   Using spreadsheets

In this exercise you will need to use a spreadsheet on a computer.

1   Jan sets up a spreadsheet for sequences.

	A	B	C	D
1	Term	Value	First difference	Second difference
2	1			
3	2			
4	3			
5	4			
6	5			
7	6			

(a)   Explain how she can get the numbers in column A without having to type them all in.

(b)   In cell B2 she enters this formula.

    =5*A2+1

What number is displayed in cell B2?

(c)   She fills down the formula in column B. This means that cell B3 has the formula

    =5*A3+1   and so on.

What number is displayed in cell B7?

(d)   In cell C3 she enters the formula

    =B3−B2

What number is displayed in cell C3?

2   Set up a spreadsheet like Jan's to display the first 20 terms of a sequence.
For each of the sequences **(a)** to **(d)** take the following steps.

(i)   Enter a formula and fill down in column B so that the first 20 terms of the sequence are displayed.

(ii)   Enter a formula and fill down in column C so that the first differences are displayed.

(iii)   Print out the results.

(iv)   On your printout, write the formulae you entered. Say which cells you entered them in.

(a) nth term $= 20 + 7n$

(b) nth term $= 7 - 0.2n$

(c)   The first term is 5. To find the next term add 2 to the previous term.

(d) $T(n) = 500 - 50n$

3   For these sequences, display and print the first 12 terms and the first, second and third differences.

(a) $n \rightarrow n^2 + 5$

(b) $n \rightarrow 2n^2$

(c) $n \rightarrow 2n^2 + 3n$

(d) $n \rightarrow 3n^2 - 5n + 2$

(e) $n \rightarrow n^3$

(f) $n \rightarrow n^3 - 5n$

6.4   Spatial patterns

You may find squared paper useful for this exercise.

1   Here is a sequence of patterns.

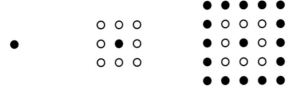

Pattern 1   Pattern 2   Pattern 3

(a)   Draw the next two patterns in the sequence.
(b)   Copy and complete this table.

Pattern number	1	2	3	4	5	6
Number of circles	2					
Number of stars	2					

(c)   How many stars are there in   (i) pattern 10   (ii) pattern 100?
(d)   How many circles are there in   (i) pattern 10   (ii) the nth pattern?

2   Look at these patterns.

Pattern 1   Pattern 2   Pattern 3

(a)   Copy and complete this table.

Pattern number	1	2	3	4	5	6
Total number of dots in pattern	1	9				
Number of dots added from previous pattern	–	8				
Number of black dots	1	1				
Number of white dots	0	8				

(b)   How many dots are added to the 10th pattern to make the 11th pattern?
(c)   How many dots are added to the nth pattern to make the $(n + 1)$th pattern?
(d)   What is special about the numbers in the 'Total number of dots' row in the table?
(e)   What is the total number of dots in   (i) the 13th   (ii) the nth pattern?
(f)   What patterns can you find in the numbers of black dots and white dots?

7 Circles

7.1 Circumference and diameter

Use π = 3.14 in questions 1 to 6. Give your answers to 2 decimal places where necessary.

1 Use measurements to calculate the circumferences of these circles.

(a)

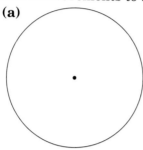

(b)

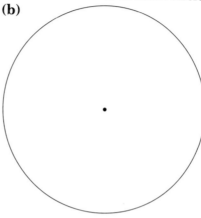

2 What length of wire is needed to make each of these rings?
   (a) Diameter 2 cm **(b)** Diameter 22 mm **(c)** Radius 9 mm

3 A piece of wire 47.5 cm long is bent into a circle.
Calculate the diameter of the circle.

4 An odometer is used by surveyors to measure distances.
It has a wheel which turns once as it moves 1 metre along the ground.
Calculate the diameter of the wheel. Give your answer to the nearest centimetre.

5 The diameter of a 2p piece is 26 mm.
   (a) Find its circumference.
   (b) How could you check your answer practically?

6 The distance round the trunk of a large tree is 3.5 m.
What is its diameter?

7 Computers are used to calculate π to over 206 158 430 000 places.
Here is π to 100 decimal places.

3.1415926535 8979323846 2643383279 5028841971 6939937510 5820974944 5923078164
0628620899 8628034825

Calculate the values of π given by these approximations. (Do not round your answers.)
Which one is best?

   (a) $\frac{355}{113}$ **(b)** $\sqrt{2} + \sqrt{3}$ **(c)** $4\left(\frac{8}{9}\right)^2$ **(d)** $\frac{99^2}{2206\sqrt{2}}$

7.2   Area of a circle

Use $\pi = 3.14$ to calculate the answers in this exercise.

1 Find the area of each of these circles.
    (a)   radius = 4 m   **(b)**   radius = 0.5 m   **(c)**   diameter = 8 cm
    (d)   diameter = 0.1 cm   **(e)**   circumference = 60 cm   **(f)**   circumference = 0.2 m

2 For each of these sectors calculate   **(i)** the area   **(ii)** the perimeter.

  (a)
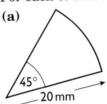

  (b)
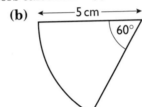

  (c)
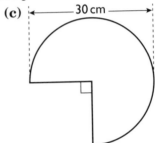

3 A grass roundabout is circular in shape. It has a diameter of 25 m.
It takes 60 g of grass seed to cover a square metre.
How many 1 kg bags of grass seed will be needed to seed the roundabout?

4 Calculate the areas of these shapes.

  (a)
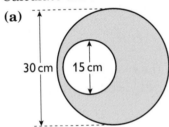

  (b)
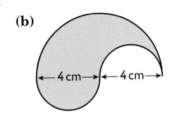

5 Calculate **(a)** the area **(b)** the perimeter of this shape.

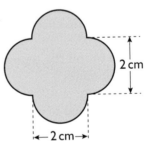

6 Use trial and improvement to find the radius, to the nearest centimetre, of a circle with an area of 1000 cm².

7 Carla wants to make a circular pen for her pet rabbits.
She has 20 metres of wire netting.
What is **(a)** the diameter **(b)** the area of the largest pen she can make?

8 **Investigation** ───────────────────────────────────────

    Explore the sites *www.expage.com.piinfo* and *www.wpdpi.com / pi.shtml*.
    The first has an interesting scavenger hunt based on π.

7.3   Circle constructions

For questions 1, 3 and 4 in this exercise you must only use a straight edge (a ruler – but not using its scale to measure lengths) and a pair of compasses. In question 2 you will also need a protractor.

When drawing constructions always leave your construction lines in – don't rub them out unless you are told to.

1   **(a) (i)**   Construct a square.
         (ii)   Draw the circle that goes through the vertices of the square.
    (b) (i)   Construct an isosceles right-angled triangle.
         (ii)   Draw the circle that goes through the vertices of the triangle.
    (c) (i)   Construct any right-angled triangle.
         (ii)   Draw the circle that goes through the vertices of the triangle.

2   Look carefully at a 50p coin.
Write down three observations about its geometry.
Now do a scale drawing of a 50p coin.
(You will need to use a protractor.)

You might like to look on the internet for some other interesting geometrical facts about this coin.

3   **(a)**   Draw a circle with radius 5 cm.
    (b)   Construct an equilateral triangle with vertices on your circle.
    (c)   Construct an equilateral triangle enclosing your circle.

4   **(a)**   Draw any quadrilateral and construct squares on each side facing outwards.
    (b)   What do you notice about the straight lines joining the centres of opposite squares?

If you think before you draw you may be able to save yourself some work!

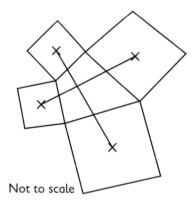

Not to scale

5   **Investigation**

Visit the website *www.members.shaw.ca / ron.blond / Circle.Geom2.APPLET /*.
Experiment with the tangents and circle there.
Write down anything interesting you find out about tangents and circles.
If you notice something which works all the time with the program, does this prove that it is true all the time?

8 Ratio

8.1 Ratio

1 Simplify these ratios.
- **(a)** $25 : 200$
- **(b)** $16 : 60$
- **(c)** $12 : 72 : 144$
- **(d)** $150 : 425$
- **(e)** $248 : 372 : 620$
- **(f)** $261 : 435 : 348$
- **(g)** $3\frac{3}{4} : 6\frac{1}{4}$
- **(h)** $4\frac{1}{2} : 7\frac{1}{5}$
- **(i)** $0.005 : 0.1$
- **(j)** $2.2 : 0.011$
- **(k)** $5 \text{ minutes} : 3 \text{ hours}$
- **(l)** $3 \text{ km} : 10 \text{ cm}$

2 Find the missing quantities in these ratios.
- **(a)** $3 : 4 = \ldots : 36$
- **(b)** $7 : 11 = 35 : \ldots$
- **(c)** $1 : 15 = \ldots : 90$
- **(d)** $3.5 : 6 = 14 : \ldots$
- **(e)** $2.25 : \ldots = 36 : 80$
- **(f)** $1 : \ldots = 2 \text{ cm} : 5 \text{ km}$

3 A map has a scale of $1 : 25\,000$.
Which of these ratios is the same as the map scale?
- **(a)** $1 \text{ cm} : 2.5 \text{ km}$
- **(b)** $1 \text{ cm} : 25 \text{ m}$
- **(c)** $4 \text{ cm} : 1 \text{ km}$
- **(d)** $25 \text{ cm} : 1 \text{ km}$
- **(e)** $1 \text{ cm} : 250 \text{ m}$

4 A map has a scale of $2 \text{ cm} : 3 \text{ km}$.
- **(a)** What distances on the map are represented by these lengths?
  - **(i)** 10 cm
  - **(ii)** 4.6 cm
  - **(iii)** 12.7 cm
- **(b)** What lengths on the map represent these distances?
  - **(i)** 36 km
  - **(ii)** 8.1 km
  - **(iii)** 31.2 km
- **(c)** Write the scale in the form $1 : n$.

5 Jasmine mixes orange juice and lemonade in the ratio $2 : 5$ to make fizzy orange.
- **(a)** How much lemonade does she need to mix with 30 ml of orange juice?
- **(b)** How much orange juice does she need to mix with 1 litre of lemonade?
- **(c)** How much of each does she mix to make 3.5 litres of fizzy orange?

8.2   Ratios and similar figures

1 Which of the following rectangles are an enlargement of this one?

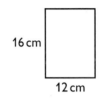
16 cm
12 cm

(a) 80 cm / 48 cm
(b) 48 mm / 36 mm
(c) 40 cm / 30 cm
(d) 30 mm / 48 mm
(e) 24 cm / 32 cm

2 **(a)** The following rectangles are similar to this one. Find the lengths marked x, y and z.

30 cm
18 cm

72 cm
x

165 cm
y

117 m
z

(b) One side of another similar rectangle is 270 cm. What can the length of the other side be?

3 A photograph is 8 cm by 12 cm.
(a) These are enlargements. Calculate the lengths marked x and y.

8 cm
A   12 cm

x
B   36 cm

y
C   40 cm

(b) Calculate the areas of photographs A, B and C.
(c) The ratio of the lengths of A and B is 12 : 36. Write this ratio in its simplest form.
(d) Find the ratio of the areas of A and B in its simplest form.
(e) What is the ratio of the lengths of A and C in its simplest form?
(f) What is the ratio of the areas of A and C in its simplest form?

4 X and Y are two cubes.
(a) What is the ratio of the lengths of X and Y in its simplest form?
(b) Write down the ratio of the volumes of X and Y and simplify your answer.
(c) How can the answer to **(b)** be obtained from your answer to **(a)**?

X
4 cm

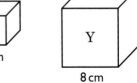
Y
8 cm

5 Two boxes are similar in shape. Their lengths are in the ratio $1 : 2$.
The volume of the larger one is $720\,\text{cm}^3$.
Find the volume of the smaller one.

6 A park has an area of $240\,000\,\text{m}^2$. There is a path
from the gate to the pond of length $250\,\text{m}$.
A map of the park has a scale of $1 : 5000$.
  (a) Calculate the length on the map of the path
      from the gate to the pond.
  (b) Calculate the area on the map of the park.

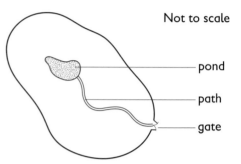

7 Two cylindrical tanks are similar in shape. Their volumes are $600\,000\,\text{cm}^3$ and $16.2\,\text{m}^3$.
The height of the larger one is $7.47\,\text{m}$.
Find the height, in metres, of the smaller one.

8.3   Proportionality

You will need graph paper for this exercise.

1 (a) b is proportional to a. Write this in symbols.
  (b) When $b = 3$, $a = 24$.
     Find the constant of proportionality and hence the law of variation.
  (c) (i) Find b when $a = 68$.   (ii) Find a when $b = 5$.

2 (a) y is proportional to c. Write this in symbols.
  (b) When $c = 5$, $y = 32$.
     Find the constant of proportionality and hence the law of variation.
  (c) (i) Find y when $c = 12$.   (ii) Find c when $y = 70.4$.

3 (a) y is proportional to x^2. Write this in symbols.
  (b) When $x = 3$, $y = 54$.
     Find the constant of proportionality and hence the law of variation.
  (c) (i) Find y when $x = 8$.   (ii) Find x when $y = 150$.

4 (a) $A \propto \sqrt{x}$. Write this as an equation.
  (b) When $x = 100$, $A = 3$.
     Find the constant of proportionality and hence the law of variation.
  (c) (i) Find A when $x = 25$.
     (ii) Find A when $x = 90.4$. Give your answer to 2 decimal places.
     (iii) Find x when $A = 5.5$. Give your answer to the nearest whole number.

5 (a) $V \propto \dfrac{1}{r}$ and when $r = 50$, $V = 4.8$. Find the law of variation.

  (b) (i) Find V when $r = 5$.   (ii) Find r when $V = 480$.

6 (a) Copy and complete this table.

x	0	1	2	3	4
x^2					
y	0	4.2	16.8	37.8	67.2

  (b) Draw axes taking the horizontal axis from 0 to 20 and the vertical axis from 0 to 80.
  (c) Plot the points from the table. Plot the x^2 value on the horizontal axis and the y value on the vertical axis. What do you notice?
  (d) (i) Write down the equation connecting x and y.
     (ii) Write down a proportionality statement connecting x and y.

7 **Investigation**

F varies directly as m.
(a) When $m = 20$, $F = 196$. Find the law of variation.
(b) Copy and complete this table.

m	10		150	
F		490		1020

(c) (i) Find out about Sir Isaac Newton and how he is connected with this law.
   (ii) What is weight? How can somebody be 'weightless'?

9 Simultaneous equations

9.1 Solving pairs of equations

1 (a) Copy and complete this table.

x	0	1	2	3	4
$2x$	0				8
-1	-1				-1
$y = 2x - 1$	-1				7

(b) Make a table for the line $y = x + 1$.
(c) Draw the lines $y = 2x - 1$ and $y = x + 1$ on the same axes.
(d) Use your graph to solve these simultaneous equations.

$$y = 2x - 1$$
$$y = x + 1$$

2 (a) Copy and complete this table.

x	0	1	2	3	4
$y = 2x + 1$	1			7	

(b) Make a table for the line $y = x + 2$.
(c) Draw the lines $y = 2x + 1$ and $y = x + 2$ on the same axes.
(d) Use your graph to solve these simultaneous equations.

$$y = 2x + 1$$
$$y = x + 2$$

3 Use algebra to solve the following pairs of equations.

(a) $y = x$
$x + 4y = 10$

(b) $p = q$
$7p + q = 24$

(c) $a = 2b$
$2a + 3b = 14$

(d) $e = 2f$
$5e - 5f = 30$

(e) $m = 3n$
$m + 6n = 27$

(f) $u = v + 8$
$u + 2v = 20$

(g) $y = 4 - x$
$4x + y = 10$

(h) $v = w$
$6v = 22 - 5w$

(i) $a = 8b$
$a + 5 = 6b + 7$

(j) $c = 3d$
$2c - 7 = d + 3$

(k) $e = 7 - f$
$3e + 2f = 19$

(l) $2g = 3h$
$2g + 5h = 32$

(m) $3p = 5q$
$6p - 4q = 18$

(n) $3x = 2y - 1$
$6x + 2y = 28$

(o) $2m = 5n$
$4m - 5 = 21 - 3n$

4 Sandra buys four crayons and a notepad. She pays 90p.
(a) Write down an equation for what Sandra buys.
Use c pence for the cost of one crayon and n pence for the cost of a notepad.
(b) Sandra writes down the equation $n = 5c$.
What does this equation mean?
(c) Solve the two equations to find the cost of a crayon and the cost of a notepad.

5 (a) At Avonford zoo the price of an adult ticket is twice the price of a child's ticket.
Write this information as an equation. Use £a for the price of an adult ticket and £c for the price of a child's ticket.
(b) Mr and Mrs Rees and their three children pay £28 to visit the zoo.
Write this information as an equation in terms of a and c.
(c) Solve your equations. What are the prices of an adult's ticket and a child's ticket?

9.2   Simultaneous equations

1 Solve the following equations.

(a) $3a + 4b = 11$
     $3a + b = 5$

(b) $2c + 5d = 11$
     $2c + 3d = 9$

(c) $6e + 4f = 8$
     $6e + f = 2$

(d) $6g + 5h = 17$
     $2g + 5h = 9$

(e) $10j + 2k = 74$
     $4j + 2k = 32$

(f) $7m + 3n = 76$
     $4m + 3n = 46$

(g) $8p + 6q = 52$
     $3p + 6q = 27$

(h) $2r + 3t = 17$
     $2r + 5t = 23$

(i) $6u + 3v = 51$
     $u + 3v = 21$

(j) $5w + x = 44$
     $5w + 7x = 68$

(k) $3y + 4z = 110$
     $5y + 4z = 130$

(l) $5x + 2y = 53$
     $5x + 8y = 77$

2 Colin buys two shirts and three pairs of trousers. He spends £46.
(a) Write an equation for what Colin buys. Use s for the cost of a shirt and t for the cost of a pair of trousers.

Trevor buys four shirts and three pairs of trousers. He spends £56.
(b) Write a second equation in terms of s and t.
(c) Solve your two equations. What are the cost of a shirt and the cost of a pair of trousers?

3 Helen buys five bread rolls and two cakes for £1.80.
(a) Write an equation for what Helen buys. Use r pence for the cost of a bread roll and c pence for the cost of a cake.
     (Hint: Write 180 pence rather than £1.80.)

Samantha buys three bread rolls and two cakes for £1.48 in the same shop.
(b) Write a second equation in r and c.
(c) Solve the two equations. What are the cost of one bread roll and the cost of one cake?

4 This table shows the bills for two guests at a seaside hotel.

	Number of nights bed and breakfast	Number of evening meals	Total bill (in £)
Aminah	5	2	305
Sally	3	2	195

(a) Write down two equations for this information. Use £n for the cost of bed and breakfast for one night and £m for the cost of an evening meal.
(b) Solve your two equations to find n and m.
(c) Gary stays at the same hotel for seven nights and has four evening meals. How much does Gary's bill come to?

9.3   Solving simultaneous equations

1 Solve these simultaneous equations by adding the two equations together.

(a) $4a + 3b = 11$
      $3a - 3b = 3$

(b) $2c - 5d = 3$
      $4c + 5d = 21$

(c) $5e + 4f = 15$
      $3e - 4f = 9$

(d) $g - 3h = 2$
      $2g + 3h = 22$

(e) $4j - 3k = 8$
      $4j + 3k = 32$

(f) $7m - 5n = 24$
      $3m + 5n = 46$

(g) $8p + q = 26$
      $8p - q = 6$

(h) $5r - 7t = 19$
      $2r + 7t = 37$

(i) $12u + 5v = 53$
      $8u - 5v = 27$

2 Simplify the following.

(a) $4x - 7x$

(b) $4x - (-7x)$

(c) $-8x - 5x$

(d) $-8x - (-5x)$

(e) $2x - (-6x)$

(f) $-x - 3x$

(g) $-9x - (-4x)$

(h) $6x - x$

(i) $-x - (-5x)$

(j) $2x - 5x$

(k) $10x - (-6x)$

(l) $-6x - x$

3 Solve the following simultaneous equations by subtracting one from the other.

(a) $4x - 3y = 5$
      $3x - 3y = 3$

(b) $4a + 5b = 22$
      $4a - 5b = 2$

(c) $4e - 4f = 32$
      $e - 4f = 2$

(d) $2p - 3q = 3$
      $7p - 3q = 33$

(e) $6j - 3k = 24$
      $6j + k = 32$

(f) $8x + 2y = 14$
      $8x + 4y = 20$

(g) $11c - 3d = 29$
      $6c - 3d = 9$

(h) $5x + 3y = 25$
      $5x - 2y = 0$

(i) $9u - 3v = 21$
      $9u - 7v = 13$

4 Solve the following simultaneous equations.
In each case you will need to decide whether to add or subtract.

(a) $2a + 5b = 9$
      $3a - 5b = 1$

(b) $4c - 5d = 6$
      $3c + 5d = 22$

(c) $5e + 7f = 19$
      $5e + 2f = 9$

(d) $5g - 4h = 15$
      $3g - 4h = 9$

(e) $9j - 2k = 1$
      $9j + 3k = 21$

(f) $6m + 5n = 40$
      $6m - 2n = 26$

(g) $8p - 7q = 17$
      $3p - 7q = 2$

(h) $6r + 5t = 32$
      $r + 5t = 22$

(i) $13u + 4v = 46$
      $13u - 2v = 16$

(j) $4w + 3x = 29$
      $4w + 5x = 43$

(k) $4y - 3z = 0$
      $4y + 5z = 32$

(l) $11x - 2y = 25$
      $11x - 8y = 1$

5 Helen is Katherine's older sister. Their ages added together give 36.
The difference between their ages is 4.

(a) Using h years for Helen's age and k years for Katherine's age write the information as two equations.

(b) Solve your equations. What are the ages of Helen and Katherine?

6 Maria has some ten pence and five pence coins in her purse.
Use t for the number of ten pence coins and f for the number of five pence coins.

(a) Write an expression, in terms of t, for the value of the ten pence coins in her purse.

(b) Write an expression, in terms of f, for the value of the five pence coins in her purse.

The value of all the coins is 85p.

(c) Write an equation, in terms of t and f, to represent this information.

Maria has 11 coins altogether.

(d) Write a second equation in terms of t and f.

(e) Solve your two equations. How many ten pence coins and how many five pence coins does she have?

9.4 More simultaneous equations

1 Solve these simultaneous equations.

(a) $3a + b = 14$
$2a + 3b = 14$

(b) $2c + 3d = 19$
$4c + d = 13$

(c) $4e + f = 35$
$3e + 2f = 35$

(d) $p - 3q = 2$
$3p - 4q = 16$

(e) $4r - 3t = 21$
$r - 5t = 1$

(f) $12u - 3v = 6$
$6u + 4v = 36$

(g) $2g - h = 3$
$3g + 3h = 18$

(h) $7j + 2k = 32$
$2j - 4k = 0$

(i) $2m + 5n = 23$
$5m - 2n = 14$

(j) $4x + 3y = 25$
$3x + 4y = 31$

(k) $2a + 7b = 30$
$3a - 2b = 20$

(l) $11g - 6h = 53$
$3g - 4h = 5$

(m) $2w - 3x = 1$
$5w + 2x = 31$

(n) $4y + 3z = 32$
$6y - 5z = 10$

(o) $8x - 4y = 40$
$3x - 2y = 10$

2 Huma buys six pencils and two rubbers for 92p.
Simon buys five pencils and three rubbers for 90p.

(a) Write two equations for this information. Use p pence for the cost of a pencil and r pence for the cost of a rubber.

(b) Find the cost of one pencil and the cost of one rubber.

3 Look at these triangles.

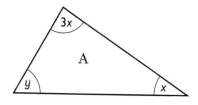
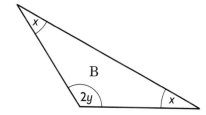

(a) Write an equation for the angles in triangle A.
(b) Write an equation for the angles in triangle B.
(c) Solve your two equations to find the values of x and y.
(d) Use your answers to (c) to find the angles of both triangles.

4 The perimeter of the pentagon is 18 cm.
The perimeter of the octagon is 34 cm.

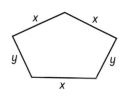
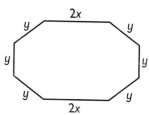

(a) Write an equation for the perimeter of the pentagon.
(b) Write an equation for the perimeter of the octagon.
(c) Solve the two equations.
(d) Find the lengths of the sides of both shapes.

10 Fractions

10.1 The language of fractions

1 Work out the following.

(a) $\frac{1}{4} + \frac{2}{5}$ (b) $\frac{7}{8} - \frac{1}{6}$ (c) $\frac{3}{7} + \frac{1}{2}$ (d) $\frac{3}{5} \times \frac{2}{3}$ (e) $\frac{4}{7} \div \frac{2}{3}$

2 Write each of these fractions in its lowest terms.

(a) $\frac{175}{450}$ (b) $\frac{36x}{64x}$ (c) $\frac{3a}{12a}$ (d) $\frac{8b}{16c}$

(e) $\frac{40e^2 f}{72ef^3}$ (f) $\frac{x^3 y^2 z}{x^5 y z^3}$ (g) $\frac{9a + 6b}{15a + 10b}$

3 Simplify each of the following expressions.

(a) $\frac{1}{3} + \frac{1}{2b}$ (b) $\frac{5}{2x} - \frac{1}{x}$ (c) $\frac{x}{y} \times \frac{3}{y}$ (d) $\frac{10}{x} \div \frac{2}{x}$ (e) $\frac{3a^2 b}{b^3} \times \frac{6ab}{5a^2 b^2}$

4 Write down the reciprocal of each of these fractions or expressions.

(a) $\frac{1}{3}$ (b) $\frac{1}{2b}$ (c) $2\frac{1}{2}$ (d) $\frac{1}{2a - b}$ (e) $4x - y$ (f) x^2

5 (a) Copy this table.

Number	Reciprocal	Decimal	Recurring digits
3			
7			
9			
11			
13			

(b) Complete the second column with the reciprocal of the number in the first column.
(c) Complete the third column with the reciprocal written as a decimal.
(d) Complete the last column with the number of recurring digits in the decimal.

10.2 Working with mixed numbers

1 Work out the following.

(a) $2\frac{1}{2} + 1\frac{3}{4}$ (b) $1\frac{1}{3} + 3\frac{1}{2}$ (c) $4\frac{1}{5} + 3\frac{2}{3}$ (d) $2\frac{3}{4} + 3\frac{5}{6}$ (e) $5\frac{1}{8} + 3\frac{2}{5}$

2 Work out the following.

(a) $2\frac{3}{4} - 1\frac{1}{2}$ (b) $3\frac{3}{4} - 1\frac{2}{3}$ (c) $7\frac{1}{2} - 3\frac{3}{5}$ (d) $4\frac{2}{3} - 2\frac{9}{10}$ (e) $5\frac{1}{4} - 3\frac{3}{5}$

3 Work out the following.

(a) $1\frac{1}{13} \times 2\frac{1}{2}$ (b) $1\frac{7}{8} \times 3\frac{2}{3}$ (c) $2\frac{7}{10} \times 1\frac{1}{6}$ (d) $5\frac{1}{4} \times 4\frac{4}{7}$ (e) $5\frac{1}{8} \times 3\frac{1}{5}$

4 Work out the following.

(a) $3\frac{1}{2} \div 1\frac{3}{4}$ (b) $1\frac{4}{5} \div 2\frac{1}{2}$ (c) $4\frac{2}{3} \div 2\frac{1}{6}$ (d) $3\frac{3}{7} \div 5\frac{4}{5}$ (e) $5\frac{1}{5} \div 11\frac{7}{10}$

5 For each of these sequences write down **(i)** the rule **(ii)** the next two terms.

(a) $1\frac{1}{2}, 2\frac{1}{4}, 3, 3\frac{3}{4}, ..., ...$

(b) $\frac{2}{3}, 2, 3\frac{1}{3}, 4\frac{2}{3}, ..., ...$

(c) $1\frac{1}{2}, 2\frac{3}{10}, 3\frac{1}{10}, 3\frac{9}{10}, ..., ...$

(d) $6\frac{5}{6}, 6\frac{1}{3}, 5\frac{5}{6}, 5\frac{1}{3}, ..., ...$

(e) $10\frac{1}{2}, 9\frac{1}{10}, 7\frac{7}{10}, 6\frac{3}{10}, ..., ...$

6 Work out these powers and square roots.

(a) $\left(1\frac{1}{2}\right)^2$ (b) $\left(1\frac{1}{2}\right)^3$ (c) $\left(2\frac{1}{4}\right)^2$ (d) $\sqrt{\frac{9}{25}}$ (e) $\sqrt{2\frac{1}{4}}$ (f) $\sqrt{1\frac{7}{9}}$

7 (a) Simplify the ratio $2\frac{1}{4} : 4\frac{1}{2} : 1\frac{1}{8}$.

(b) Use your answer to **(a)** to divide £6300 in the ratio $2\frac{1}{4} : 4\frac{1}{2} : 1\frac{1}{8}$.

Graphs

11.1 Mapping diagrams

You will need squared paper for this exercise.

1 For each of the following mappings
  (i) construct a table of values taking values of x from 0 to 6
  (ii) draw the mapping diagram.
  (a) $x \rightarrow 2x + 1$ **(b)** $y = 3x - 2$ **(c)** $y = 2x$ **(d)** $x \rightarrow 4(x - 1)$
  (e) $y = 8 - \frac{1}{2}x$ **(f)** $x \rightarrow 7 + 2x$ **(g)** $x \rightarrow \dfrac{2x + 4}{8}$ **(h)** $y = 2.5x - 4$
  (i) $y = \dfrac{x}{10} + 2$ **(j)** $x \rightarrow \dfrac{2x - 3}{5}$

2 A water company uses the formula $C = 0.9n + 16$ to work out the half-yearly cost, £C, of supplying n m³ of water.
  (a) Work out the cost of supplying 20 m³ of water.
  (b) Copy and complete this table.

n	10	20	30	40	50
$0.9n$	9				
$+16$	16				
$C = 0.9n + 16$	25				

  (c) Draw the mapping diagram.
  (d) Frank's last bill came to £56.50. How many cubic metres of water did he use?

3 A hire firm uses the formula $C = 24D + 10$ to work out the cost, £C, of hiring a car for D days.
  (a) Copy and complete this table.

D	2	4	6	8	10
$24D$					240
$+10$					10
$C = 24D + 10$					250

  (b) Draw the mapping diagram.
  (c) Peggy spends £226 on hiring a car. For how many days does she hire the car?
  (d) How much does the firm charge for each extra day?

4 The width, M centimetres, of material needed to make a pair of curtains for a window of width W centimetres is given by the formula $M = \dfrac{5W}{2} + 40$.
  (a) Copy and complete this table.

W	50	60	70	80	90
$\dfrac{5W}{2}$	125				
$+40$	40				
$M = \dfrac{5W}{2} + 40$	165				

  (b) Draw the mapping diagram.
  (c) Peter uses material 365 cm wide to make a pair of curtains for his dining room. How wide is his dining room window?

11.2 Inverse mappings

1 Write down the inverse function of each of the following.

(a) $y = 3x$ (b) $y = x + 20$ (c) $y = x - 8$ (d) $x \rightarrow x + 7$

(e) $x \rightarrow x - 15$ (f) $x \rightarrow \dfrac{x}{5}$ (g) $y = \dfrac{x}{50}$ (h) $y = x - 6$

2 Use the flow diagram method to find the formula for the inverse function of each of the following.

(a) $y = 2x + 7$ (b) $y = 7 + 5x$ (c) $x \rightarrow 3x - 8$ (d) $x \rightarrow 9 + 12x$

(e) $x \rightarrow 1 + 6x$ (f) $y = 4x - 15$ (g) $y = 8 + 4x$ (h) $y = 5x - 6$

3 Find the formula for the inverse of each of the following mappings.

(a) $y = \frac{1}{4}x + 3$ (b) $x \rightarrow \frac{1}{5}x - 8$ (c) $x \rightarrow 2(x - 9)$ (d) $y = 7(x + 2)$

(e) $y = \dfrac{3x}{5}$ (f) $x \rightarrow \frac{2}{3}x - 5$ (g) $y = \frac{1}{3}(x - 1)$ (h) $y = \frac{1}{10}(9 + x)$

4 Find the formula for the inverse of each of the following mappings.

(a) $y = 7x + 4$ (b) $y = \dfrac{x + 12}{4}$ (c) $y = \dfrac{x - 6}{5}$ (d) $y = 7(x + 2)$

(e) $y = \frac{3}{4}x$ (f) $x \rightarrow \frac{1}{2}x - 5$ (g) $y = \frac{1}{2}(x - 5)$ (h) $y = \frac{1}{4}(8 + x)$

5 Sally is making lines of pentagons using matchsticks. She records the number of matchsticks she needs in this table.

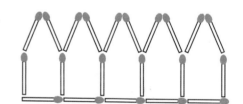

Number of pentagons, p	Number of matchsticks, m
1	5
2	9
3	
4	
5	
⋮	⋮

(a) Write down a formula for m in terms of p.
(b) What is the value of m when p is 80?
(c) Find the formula for p in terms of m.
(d) What is the value of p when m is 89?

11.3 Plotting graphs

You will need squared paper or graph paper for this exercise.

1 **(a)** Taking x from -2 to 6 and y from -5 to 11, plot the lines $y = x + 1$ and $y = 7 - 2x$ on the same axes.
   (b) Write down the co-ordinates of
      A where these lines cross
      B where the line $y = x + 1$ crosses the y axis
      C where the line $y = 7 - 2x$ crosses the y axis.
   (c) What is the area of triangle ABC?

2 **(a)** Plot the lines $y = 2x + 5$ and $y = 2x - 1$ on the same axes for values of x from -3 to 5.
   (b) How are these lines related?
   (c) Write the equations of three more lines that have the same relationship to the lines already drawn.

3 **(a)** Using the same scale on both axes plot the lines $y = 2x + 1$ and $y = 11 - \frac{1}{2}x$ for values of x from -4 to 6.
   (b) How are these lines related?

4 Each of the points in list A lies on one of the lines in list B.
   Match each point to one of the lines.

List A		List B	
(2, 13)	(−2, 16)	$y = 3x - 4$	$y = x - 4$
(4, 0)	(4, 1)	$y = 8 - 5x$	$y = 9 - 2x$
(−3, −13)	(−2, 3)	$y = 10 - 3x$	$y = 4x + 5$
(−2, 18)		$y = 2x + 7$	

5 For each of these lines, find where it crosses the x and y axes and sketch its graph.
   (a) $2x + 5y = 10$ **(b)** $4x - 3y = 24$

6 Find the equations of the lines in these sketches.
   (a) 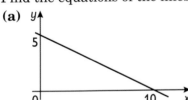   **(b)**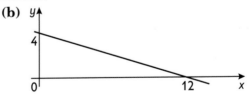

11.4 The equation of a line

You will need squared paper or graph paper for this exercise.

1 **(a)** Make a table of values for $y = 2x + 5$, taking values of x from -4 to 4.
    (b) Draw the graph.
    (c) Calculate the gradient of the line.
    (d) Write down the co-ordinates of the intercept on the y axis.

2 State the gradient and the co-ordinates of the intercept for each of these lines.
    (a) $y = 2x + 7$ **(b)** $y = 7 - 5x$ **(c)** $y = 3x - 8$ **(d)** $y = 1 + 12x$
    (e) $y = 5 - 6x$ **(f)** $y = -4x$ **(g)** $y = 8 + x$ **(h)** $y = 9x - 6$

3 **(a)** Plot the line $2x + 5y = 20$ for values of x from 0 to 12.
    (b) What is the gradient?
    (c) What are the co-ordinates of the points where it crosses the axes?

4 **(a)** State the gradient and the co-ordinates of the intercept of the lines in these sketches.

(i) 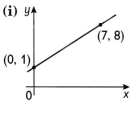   **(ii)** 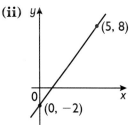   **(iii)**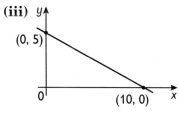

    (b) Write down the equations of the lines in **(a)**.

5 **(a)** Plot the line that passes through the points $(1, 5)$ and $(4, 11)$.
    (b) What are the co-ordinates of the intercept?
    (c) Calculate the gradient.
    (d) Hence, write down the equation of the line.

6 State the gradient and the co-ordinates of the intercept of each of these lines.
    (a) $y + 3x = 7$ **(b)** $y - 4x = 8$ **(c)** $5x + y = 10$ **(d)** $2x - y = 12$

7 Take values of x from -6 to 10 and draw the line with gradient 0.25 and intercept 2.

8 **(a)** Draw a set of axes from -4 to 16 for both x and y and draw the quadrilateral with these vertices.

        $P(-2, 1)$ $Q(3, 11)$ $R(12, 14)$ $S(4, -2)$

    (b) Work out the gradient of each of these lines.
        (i) PQ   **(ii)** QR   **(iii)** SR   **(iv)** PS
    (c) Describe the quadrilateral PQRS.

11.5 Curves

You will need graph paper for this exercise.

1 **(a)** Copy and complete this table for $y = x^2 + 4$.

x	-4	-3	-2	-1	0	1	2	3	4
x^2	16								
$+4$	$+4$								
$y = x^2 + 4$	20								

   (b) Plot the points and join them with a smooth curve.
   (c) Use your graph to estimate the value of y when $x = 3.5$.
   (d) Use your graph to estimate the value of x when $y = 14$.

2 **(a)** Copy and complete this table for $y = 2x^2 - 7$.

x	-3	-2	-1	0	1	2	3
$2x^2$	18						
-7	-7						
$y = 2x^2 - 7$	11						

   (b) Plot the points and join them with a smooth curve.
   (c) Use your graph to estimate the value of x when $y = 10$.
   (d) On the same axes draw the line $y = 6$.
   (e) Use your graph to solve the equation $2x^2 - 7 = 6$.

3 **(a)** Copy and complete this table for $y = x^2 + 3x$.

x	-5	-4	-3	-2	-1	0	1	2
x^2	25							
$+3x$	-15							
$y = x^2 + 3x$	10							

   (b) Plot the points and join them with a smooth curve.
   (c) On the same axes draw the line $y = x$.
   (d) Use your graph to solve the equation $x^2 + 3x = x$.

4 **(a)** On the same axes draw the curve $y = (x - 1)^2$ and the line $y = x + 1$.
       Take values of x from -3 to 5.
   (b) Use your graph to solve the equation $(x - 1)^2 = x + 1$.

12 Construction and locus

12.1 Using scale drawings

You will need a ruler, a protractor and a pair of compasses for this exercise.

1 A flag pole is 30 feet tall. It is supported by two guy ropes both attached to the ground 5 feet from the base of the pole.

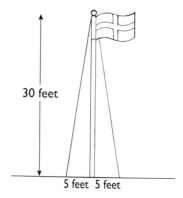

Make a scale drawing.
Use it to find the length of the guy ropes.

2 Alan is finding the height of a church spire.
He stands 20 m from the base of the spire.
From this position the angle of elevation of the top is 52°.

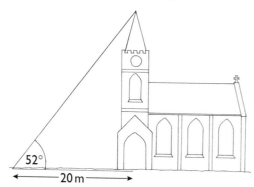

Make a scale drawing.
Use it to find the height of the spire.

3 An aircraft leaves an airport and flies north east for 150 km.
Make a scale drawing.
Use it to find how far north the aircraft has flown.

4   A buoy is 2 km due north of a lighthouse.
Jim is on a boat. He takes the bearings of the buoy and the lighthouse.
The buoy is on a bearing of 046° from the boat.
The lighthouse is on a bearing of 127° from the boat.

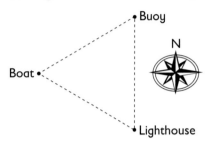

Make a scale drawing.
Find the distance of
(a)   the boat from the buoy
(b)   the boat from the lighthouse.

5   This is the sketch of the end wall of a store room.

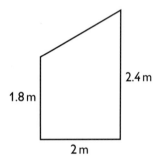

Grace wants to put a cupboard against this wall.
The cupboard is 1.5 m wide and 2 m high.
Make an accurate scale drawing.
Use it to find out if the cupboard will fit.

12.2 Congruency and similarity

You will need a ruler, a protractor and a pair of compasses for this exercise.

1 **(i)** Draw each of these triangles.
    (ii) In each case state whether the triangle is uniquely defined.
       If the triangle is not uniquely defined explain why not.
    (a) AB = 5 cm, BC = 7 cm, AC = 8 cm
    (b) $A\hat{B}C = 52°$, $B\hat{C}A = 64°$, $B\hat{A}C = 64°$
    (c) AB = 8 cm, BC = 7 cm, $C\hat{A}B = 45°$
    (d) BC = 7.5 cm, $A\hat{B}C = 72°$, $B\hat{C}A = 46°$
    (e) AB = 9 cm, BC = 6.5 cm, $A\hat{B}C = 55°$

2 Yacht A is due west of yacht C.
    The skipper of yacht A can see a buoy on a bearing of 070°.
    The skipper of yacht C can see a buoy on a bearing of 030°.
    Can it be the same buoy?

3 The sketch represents a triangular lawn next to a house.
    (a) Make a scale drawing using 1 cm to represent 5 m.
    (b) Is the triangle uniquely defined?
    (c) The lead on an electric lawnmower is 24 m long.
       There is an electric socket on the house wall 10 m from B.
       Can the lawnmower reach all points on the lawn?

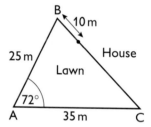

4 A buoy C is 5 km due east of buoy B.
    A boat A is 3 km from buoy B and on a bearing of 240° from buoy C.
    Make an accurate scale drawing showing the position of the boat and the buoys.
    Is the position of the boat uniquely defined?

5 **Investigation**

> In each case you are asked to draw a quadrilateral ABCD from the given information.
> **(i)** Say whether or not it is possible.
> **(ii)** If possible, construct the quadrilateral and say whether it is uniquely defined.
> **(a)** AB = 2 cm, BC = 2 cm, CD = 3 cm, DA = 10 cm
> **(b)** AB = 3 cm, BC = 4 cm, CD = 5 cm, DA = 6 cm
> **(c)** $A\hat{B}C = 72°$, $B\hat{C}D = 110°$, $C\hat{D}A = 88°$, $D\hat{A}B = 90°$
> **(d)** AB = 5 cm, $A\hat{B}C = 102°$, BC = 7 cm, CD = 6 cm, DA = 8 cm
> **(e)** AB = 7 cm, BC = 6 cm, CD = 8 cm, $A\hat{B}C = 108°$, $B\hat{C}D = 115°$

12.3 Locus

You will need tracing paper, a ruler and a pair of compasses for this exercise.

1   A goat is tethered by a 3 m chain which can slide along a fixed bar in the centre of a field.
The goat can move either side of the bar.
Make a sketch to show the area the goat can graze.

2   **(a)** Using a ruler and compasses only make an accurate drawing of triangle ABC, with
AB = 8 cm, AC = 6 cm, BÂC = 90°.
  (b) Draw the locus of a point which is
    (i)   equidistant from AB and AC
    (ii) equidistant from AC and BC
    (iii) equidistant from AB and BC.
  (c) Your three lines should meet at one point.
What can you say about that point?

3   **(a)** The diagram shows a scale drawing of
Treasure Island.
Trace the diagram and draw the loci
described to find the treasure.
The treasure is
    (i)   2.5 km from the landing stage
    (ii) 1 km from the line of trees
    (iii) less than 3 km from the hut.
  (b) Draw your own Treasure Island and
write down instructions using loci to find
the treasure.
Show the loci and the position of the
treasure on your map.

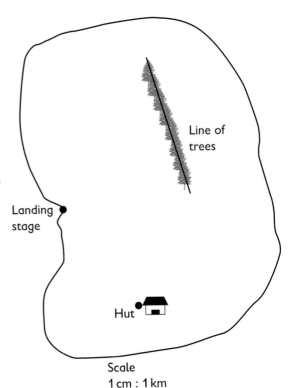

Line of trees

Landing stage

Hut

Scale
1 cm : 1 km

13 Working with data

13.1 The mean

1 Find the mean of each of the following sets of data.
  (a) The number of doughnuts sold each day at a bakers

      32   23   17   14   27   26   22

  (b) Goals scored by a school football team in ten matches

      0   3   2   1   4   1   0   4   2   1

  (c) The length, in minutes, of a telephone call made by a sales representative

      3   7   10   2   4   8   11   9   6   3
      2   4   8   15   14   10   8   7   4   7

  (d) The number of hours of sunshine at a seaside town

      7.3   4.8   1.7   6.4   5.9   7.6   6.9

  (e) The times, in seconds, of eight athletes who compete in a 100 m race

      10.34   11.35   10.68   11.71   11.82   11.02   11.95   10.81

2 The mean of this set of numbers is 20.

    13   20   18   x   24   23

Find the value of x.

3 The scores in a golf competition are summarised in this table.

Score	66	67	68	69	70	71	72	73	74
Frequency	3	2	2	7	7	9	7	9	4

  (a) How many players took part in the competition?
  (b) Calculate the mean score in the competition.

4 A class of students were asked how many brothers and sisters they each had.
The results are summarised in this bar chart.

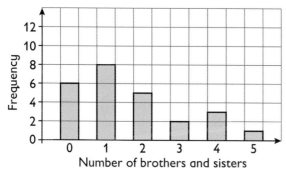

  (a) Make a frequency table for these data.
  (b) Find the mean number of brothers and sisters for this class.
  (c) What is the average number of children per family for this class?

13.2 Median, mode and range

1 For the following sets of data find **(i)** the median **(ii)** the range.
(a) The scores on a die, rolled nine times

   4   6   2   3   2   4   1   1   4

(b) The number of bruised peaches in each of eight trays

   1   2   0   5   1   4   5   3

(c) The height, in centimetres, of 12 plants

   4.3   5.2   4.1   3.5   5.2   4.8
   5.3   4.8   3.7   4.1   4.5   5.0

(d) The maximum temperature one week in winter

   3   −7   5   −6   0   −9   −7

2 These are the shoe sizes of the members of a hockey team.

   7   7   5   8   7   6   6   7   8   6   7

(a) Find
   (i)   the mean shoe size
   (ii) the median shoe size
   (iii) the mode of the shoe sizes.
(b) Which average best describes the data?
   Explain your answer.

3 The bar chart summarises the number of goals scored by the school football team in each of their matches.

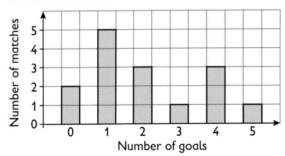

(a) What is the mode of the number of goals scored?
(b) What is the median number of goals scored?
(c) The team are about to play a cup match and want to scare the opposition.
   Which do they talk about, the mode or the median?

4 The median of these numbers is 4.

   7   2   5   6 x 1

Find the value of x.

5 The median weight of a group of four boys is 74 kg.
The range of their weights is 8 kg.
The mode is 73 kg.
What are the weights of the four boys?

13.3 Stem-and-leaf diagrams

1 These are the lengths, in centimetres, of fish caught in a fishing contest.

51	23	14	27	24	39	50	48	30	27
31	36	42	35	31	26	17	27	18	45
12	34	41	44	37	32	21	18	29	

(a) Make an ordered stem-and-leaf diagram of the results. Remember to use a key.
(b) Use your diagram to find the median length.
(c) What is the range of the data?
(d) What percentage of the fish have a length of less than 25 cm?

2 Jack is a golfer. These are his scores for last season.

115	104	102	94	98	80	113	121	102	109
97	91	77	85	108	114	79	89	99	113
97	73	86	81	99	103	108	92	80	77

(a) Make an ordered stem-and-leaf diagram of the scores.
(b) Use your diagram to work out the median score.
(c) What fraction of the scores are below 90? Give your answer in its lowest terms.

3 A class of Year 9 students take a practice maths exam.
After four weeks of revision they take another practice exam.
The marks for each exam are shown in this back-to-back stem-and-leaf diagram.

```
      Before revision          After revision
          6  6  2  1  0 | 2 | 3  4  5
       8  7  5  4  2  2  1 | 3 | 1  3  6  8
    9  8  8  6  5  5  2  2 | 4 | 0  2  5  6  9
          8  7  6  2  2  0 | 5 | 2  3  5  7
          9  9  4  4  3  1 | 6 | 1  3  5  5  6  9
                5  3  2  0 | 7 | 0  1  3  4  4  6  8
                   9  7  3 | 8 | 0  2  3  3  6  6  7
                      5  1 | 9 | 1  2  2  4  5
```

| 9 | 5 represents a mark of 95%

(a) Find the range of scores in each exam.
(b) Find the median score in each exam.
(c) Use your answers to (a) and (b) to comment on the results of the two exams.

13.4 Estimating the mean of grouped data

1 A postman records the number of letters that he delivers to 50 shops in the town centre.

Number of letters	0–4	5–9	10–14	15–19	20–24	25–29
Number of shops	5	3	3	6	17	16

   (a) What is the modal group for these data?
   (b) What percentage of shops had fewer than ten letters delivered?
   (c) Estimate the mean number of letters delivered to each shop.

2 Sally did a survey of the ages of cars in a town centre car park. Here are her results.

Age (a years)	$0 < a \leqslant 2$	$2 < a \leqslant 5$	$5 < a \leqslant 9$	$9 < a \leqslant 12$
Number of cars	82	51	23	4

   (a) What is the modal group for these data?
   (b) In which group does the median value fall?
   (c) What percentage of cars are over 9 years old?
   (d) Calculate an estimate of the mean age of these cars.

3 For quality control, a manufacturer regularly checks the volume of cola in their $\frac{1}{2}$ litre bottles. The frequency chart shows the findings after one such check.

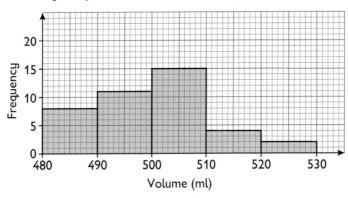

   (a) Make a frequency table for these data.
   (b) Calculate an estimate of the mean volume of cola in these bottles.
   (c) Should the manufacturer be concerned at these findings?

13.5 Estimating the median of grouped data

You will need graph paper for this exercise.

1 Martin measures the circumferences of the trees in a small wood. Here are his results.

Circumference (x cm)	Frequency
$10 < x \leqslant 20$	28
$20 < x \leqslant 30$	95
$30 < x \leqslant 40$	202
$40 < x \leqslant 50$	214
$50 < x \leqslant 60$	61

(a) Copy and complete the cumulative frequency table for these data.

Circumference (x cm)	$x \leqslant 20$	$x \leqslant 30$	$x \leqslant 40$	$x \leqslant 50$	$x \leqslant 60$
Cumulative frequency					

(b) Draw a cumulative frequency graph for these data.
(c) Use your graph to estimate the median circumference of these trees.
(d) The wood is being thinned. Trees with a circumference less than 25 cm are to be felled. Use your graph to estimate the number of trees to be felled.

2 Class 9C take a maths exam and an English exam.
The results are illustrated by these two frequency charts.

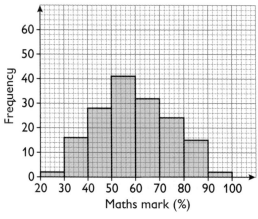 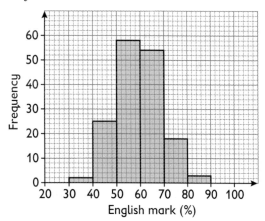

(a) Copy and complete this frequency table.

Mark ($m\%$)	Frequency (Maths)	Frequency (English)
$20 < m \leqslant 30$		
$30 < m \leqslant 40$		

(b) Make a cumulative frequency table for each set of exam scores.
(c) On the same axes, draw a cumulative frequency graph for each set of scores.
(d) Use your graph to estimate the median mark in each exam.
(e) Which exam do you think the students did better in? Explain your answer.

13.6 Estimating spread

You will need graph paper for this exercise.

1 The cumulative frequency graph
show the marks gained in an
examination taken by 400
students.

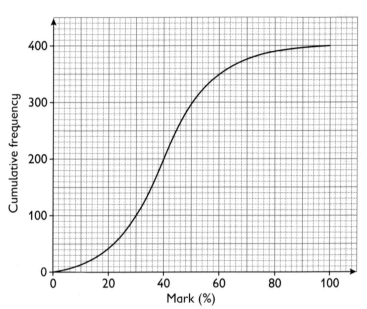

  (a) Use the graph to find
    (i) the median mark
    (ii) the lower quartile
    (iii) the upper quartile
    (iv) the interquartile range.
  (b) Students who score less
than 20% take a re-test.
Use the graph to estimate
how many students take the
re-test.
  (c) Those students who score
over 75% are awarded a
distinction.
Estimate the number of
students awarded a distinction?

2 To monitor a rare species of bird, 200 birds are captured and their wingspan is measured.
This table shows the results.

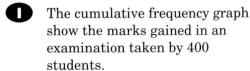

Wingspan (*w* cm)	$11 < w \leqslant 12$	$12 < w \leqslant 13$	$13 < w \leqslant 14$	$14 < w \leqslant 15$	$15 < w \leqslant 16$	$16 < w \leqslant 17$
Number of birds	14	39	67	48	22	10

  (a) Copy and complete this cumulative frequency table.

Wingspan (*w* cm)	$w \leqslant 12$	$w \leqslant 13$	$w \leqslant 14$	$w \leqslant 15$	$w \leqslant 16$	$w \leqslant 17$
Cumulative frequency						

  (b) Draw a cumulative frequency graph.
  (c) Use your graph to find
    (i) the median wingspan   **(ii)** the lower quartile
    (iii) the upper quartile   **(iv)** the interquartile range.
  (d) Those birds with a wingspan of less than 12.5 cm are given a vitamin supplement.
Estimate how many birds this is.
  (e) Those birds with a wingspan over 14.5 cm are released immediately.
Estimate how many birds this is.
  (f) In the last survey of these birds, the median was 13.1 cm and the interquartile range
was 1.2 cm.
Compare the results from the two surveys.

14 Indices and standard form

14.1 Using indices

You will need graph paper for this exercise.

1 Write the following in index form.
   (a) $5^3 \times 5^4$ **(b)** $2^2 \times 2^6$ **(c)** $8^3 \times 8^3$ **(d)** $10^4 \times 10^{10}$ **(e)** $5^3 \times 5^2 \times 5^4$
   (f) $6^4 \div 6^2$ **(g)** $22^8 \div 22^5$ **(h)** $8^3 \div 8^5$ **(i)** $20^5 \div 20^{10}$ **(j)** $\dfrac{7^4}{7^9}$

2 Write the following in index form.
   (a) $(4^3)^2$ **(b)** $(5^4)^3$ **(c)** $(6^2)^4$

3 Work out the following.
   (a) $64^{\frac{1}{2}}$ **(b)** 7^0 **(c)** 3^{-1} **(d)** $4^{-\frac{1}{2}}$ **(e)** 2^{-3}

4 Which number in each of these pairs of numbers is the larger?
   (a) 3^2 or 2^3 **(b)** 3^{-2} or 2^{-3}

5 Cells reproduce by dividing into two.

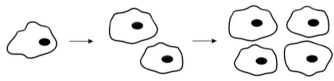

These cells increase in number two times every minute.
There is one now.
How many are there after one hour? Give your answer in index form.

6 You can use the number fact $400 = 4 \times 10^2$ to work out the square root of 400.

$$\sqrt{400} = \sqrt{4 \times 10^2} = \sqrt{4} \times \sqrt{10^2} = 2 \times 10 = 20$$

Use this method to find the square roots of these numbers.
   (a) $\sqrt{900}$ **(b)** $\sqrt{160\,000}$ **(c)** $\sqrt{25\,000\,000}$ **(d)** $\sqrt{1\,210\,000}$

7 **(a)** **(i)** Copy and complete this table for $y = 2^x$.

x	-3	-2	-1	0	1	2	3	4
$y = 2^x$	$\dfrac{1}{8}$					4		

   (ii) Draw the graph of $y = 2^x$.
   (iii) Use your graph to solve the equation $2^x = 10$.
   (b) **(i)** On another set of axes draw the graph of $y = 3^x$ taking values of x from -2 to 3.
   (ii) Use your graph to solve the equation $3^x = 20$.

14.2 Writing large and small numbers

1 Write these numbers in standard form.
  (a) 520   (b) 60   (c) 72   (d) 9000
  (e) 16 000 000   (f) 0.5   (g) 0.003   (h) 0.000 007 5

2 Write these as ordinary numbers.
  (a) 4.2×10^5 (b) 2.5×10^3 (c) 8.08×10^8 (d) 6.032×10^1
  (e) 9.9×10^{-3} (f) 4×10^{-1} (g) 2.023×10^{-4} (h) 9.8×10^{-6}

3 Write these numbers in standard form.
  (a) one hundred   (b) ten thousand   (c) one tenth
  (d) ten million   (e) five and a half billion   (f) one millionth

4 Write these numbers in order, smallest first.

  6.5×10^2 $\frac{1}{10}$ six hundred 5.7×10^2 45 000

  5.6×10^3 6.1×10^{-2} 0.0052 4×10^{-3} 10^{-2}

5 **Investigation**

How can you do these sums without using a calculator?
  (a) $(4 \times 10^2) \times (2 \times 10^3)$
  (b) $(3 \times 10^4) \times (2 \times 10^5)$
  (c) $(5 \times 10^2) \times (3 \times 10^4)$
  (d) $(8 \times 10^4) \div (2 \times 10^3)$
  (e) $(9 \times 10^4) \div (3 \times 10^2)$

14.3 Standard form on the calculator

You will need the following information in this exercise.
Light travels at approximately $3 \times 10^8 \, ms^{-1}$ and sound travels at $3.3 \times 10^2 \, ms^{-1}$.

1 $A = 3.5 \times 10^4$ $B = 6.4 \times 10^8$ $C = 4 \times 10^{-3}$ $D = 3.2 \times 10^{-5}$
Use your calculator to work out the following.
(a) $A \times B$ (b) $A \times C$ (c) $B \times D$
(d) $A + B$ (e) $B \div D$ (f) $D \div B$
(g) A^2 (h) C^4 (i) $C - D$

2   (a) $E = 1 \times 10^5$. Work out   (i) E^5 (ii) E^{20} (iii) E^{50}.
(b) What is the largest number you can use on your calculator in standard form?

3   How many times faster than sound does light travel?

4   The time between seeing the lightning and hearing the thunder can be used to estimate how far away a storm is.
(a) A storm is 1 km away. How many seconds does it take for the sound to reach you?
(b) What about when it is 1 mile away? (1 mile = 1.6 km)
(c) On seeing some lightning George counts 12 seconds before hearing the thunder. How far away from George is the storm?

5   (a) The average distance between Earth and the Sun is 1.5×10^{11} m. How long does it take light to reach Earth from the Sun?
(b) The average distance between Earth and Pluto is 5.91×10^{12} m. How long does it take light to reach Pluto from Earth?
(c) (i) It takes light about 35 minutes to reach Jupiter from Earth when they are closest. How far is Jupiter from Earth at this time?
(ii) Assuming that the Sun, Earth and Jupiter are in a straight line, calculate the distance of Jupiter from the Sun.

15 Formulae

15.1 Formulae

In this exercise use $\pi = 3.14$ and give your answer to 1 decimal place where necessary.

1 Use the following formulae. In each case give the unit of the answer.
   (a) The area of a circle, $A = \pi r^2$.
      Find A, when $r = 4.5$ (in centimetres).
   (b) The diameter of a circle, $d = \dfrac{C}{\pi}$.
      Find d, when $C = 32.5$ (in metres).
   (c) The volume of a cylinder, $V = \pi r^2 h$.
      Find V, when $r = 8.2$ and $h = 10.5$ (both in centimetres).
   (d) The time taken to complete a journey, $t = \dfrac{s}{v}$, where s is the distance travelled (in km) and v is the speed (in km h^{-1}).
      Find t when $s = 207$ and $v = 45$.
   (e) The area of a trapezium, $A = \frac{1}{2}(a + b)h$.
      Find A, when $a = 5.4$, $b = 3.6$ and $h = 2.8$ (all in metres).

2 The five parts of this question use the five formulae from question 1.
   In each case substitute in the formula to form an equation.
   Then solve the equation.
   (a) The area of a circle is 52 cm^2.
      Work out the radius.
   (b) The diameter of a circle is 6.6 cm.
      Work out the circumference.
   (c) The volume of a cylinder is 225 cm^2.
      The radius is 4 cm. Work out the height.
   (d) A car travels at 25 ms^{-1} for 42 seconds.
      How far does it travel?
   (e) The area of a trapezium is 164 cm^2.
      The parallel sides are 17 cm and 24 cm long.
      Work out the distance between them.

3 Dave is a plumber. This is how he calculates his charges.

> £25 call-out charge plus £22 per hour plus
> £0.40 per mile to travel to the job.

   (a) Write this as a formula. Use n for the number of hours, m for the number of miles and £C for the cost.
   (b) On one call-out Dave travels 25 miles and the job takes 3 hours to complete.
      How much does he charge?
   (c) On another call-out the job takes 5 hours to complete and Dave charges the customer £151. How far does he travel to the job?

15.2 Rearranging formulae

1 Make x the subject of each of these formulae.

(a) $y = 3x$

(b) $y = \frac{1}{3}x$

(c) $y = x - 4$

(d) $y = x + 4$

(e) $y = 4x + 1$

(f) $y = 2x - 5$

(g) $y = \frac{1}{2}(x + 1)$

(h) $y = \frac{1}{3}x - 5$

(i) $y = mx + c$

(j) $y = \frac{x - 4}{2}$

(k) $y = \frac{x}{4} + 5$

(l) $y = a(x + b)$

2 Make the letter in **bold** the subject of each of the following formulae.

(a) $v = u + \boldsymbol{a}t$

(b) $S = 180\boldsymbol{n} - 360$

(c) $A = 360 - \boldsymbol{B} - C - D$

(d) $C = \pi\boldsymbol{d}$

(e) $I = \frac{PRT}{100}$

(f) $I = m(\boldsymbol{v} - u)$

(g) $F = m\boldsymbol{a}$

(h) $P = mg\boldsymbol{h}$

(i) $s = \frac{1}{2}(u + v)t$

(j) $v^2 = u^2 + 2\boldsymbol{a}s$

(k) $A = 4\pi\boldsymbol{r}^2$

(l) $v^2 = \boldsymbol{u}^2 + 2as$

(m) $y = \sqrt{\dfrac{2\boldsymbol{x}}{5}}$

(n) $V = \frac{1}{3}\pi r^2 h$

(o) $E = \frac{1}{2}m\boldsymbol{v}^2$

3 Mel is a decorator. She uses the formula $C = 12n + 70$ to calculate the cost, £C, of hanging n rolls of wallpaper.
(a) Make n the subject of the formula.
(b) Mel charges a customer £166 for hanging some wallpaper.
   How many rolls does she hang?

4 The volume of a sphere is given by $V = \dfrac{4\pi r^3}{3}$.
(a) What is the volume of a sphere of radius 4 cm?
(b) Rearrange the formula to make r the subject.
(c) A ball has a volume of 5200 cm^3.
   What is the radius of the ball?
   Use $\pi = 3.14$ and give your answer to 1 decimal place.

5 (a) Find x in   (i) $\dfrac{1}{x} = \dfrac{1}{3} - \dfrac{1}{4}$ (ii) $\dfrac{1}{x} + \dfrac{2}{3} = \dfrac{4}{5}$.
(b) Make x the subject in $\dfrac{1}{x} + \dfrac{1}{p} = \dfrac{2}{q}$.

16 Accuracy

16.1 Accuracy

1 Write these numbers to the nearest 100.
(a) 478   (b) 86   (c) 5674   (d) 69 062   (e) 3829

2 Write these numbers to 2 decimal places.
(a) 2.0734   (b) 16.843   (c) 0.0473   (d) 5.392   (e) 14.977

3 Write these numbers to 3 significant figures.
(a) 53 724   (b) 521.8   (c) 0.002 066   (d) 5.2381   (e) 0.410 73

4 Write these numbers to 1 significant figure.
(a) 471   (b) 6.73   (c) 0.0274   (d) 59 621   (e) 0.000 472

5 Use your calculator to work out the following.
Write your answers to 3 significant figures.
(a) $\sqrt{10}$ (b) $5 \times \pi$ (c) $\frac{1}{7}$ (d) $\sqrt{7.4^2 + 4.5^2}$ (e) $24 \div 4.7$

6 Explain these mistakes.
(a)
> 4.545 litres to a gallon
> = 4.55 litres (3 sf)
> = 4.6 litres (2 sf)

(b)
> 16 057 = 16 060 (3 sf)

16.2 Range of values

1 (a) Jim's height is 183 cm to the nearest centimetre.
  (i)   What is the smallest possible value for Jim's height?
  (ii) What is the largest possible value for Jim's height?
  (iii) Write Jim's height as a range of values.
 (b) Write each of the following as a range of values.
  (i)   Jim weighs 70 kg (to the nearest kilogram).
  (ii) Jim receives £3 pocket money (to the nearest pound).
  (iii) The fastest time for the 100 m sprint is 12.8 seconds (to the nearest $\frac{1}{10}$ second).
  (iv) The weight of a fish is 5.6 kg (to the nearest 100 g).

2 Gwen weighs her cat as 4.5 kg. What is the lightest it could be?

3 Write each of the following measurements as a range of values and state the largest possible error for each measurement.
 (a) 6 g (to the nearest gram)
 (b) 7.5 cm (to the nearest millimetre)
 (c) 40 litres (to the nearest litre)
 (d) 18.43 m (to the nearest centimetre)
 (e) 5.7 kg (to the nearest gram)

4 Write each of the following as a range of values.
 (a) 400 (to the nearest 100)
 (b) 72 km (to the nearest kilometre)
 (c) 4.8 (correct to 1 decimal place)
 (d) 680 (correct to 2 significant figures)
 (e) 4.76 (correct to 3 significant figures)
 (f) 600 (correct to 2 significant figures)
 (g) 600 (correct to 3 significant figures)

5 Shiraz has a garden. He measures it to the nearest metre.
He wants to put grass seed all over it and put a fence around three sides.
 (a) Grass seed is sold in packets.
   Each packet contains sufficient for 100 m².
   Explain why three packets may not be enough to seed his garden.
 (b) What length of fencing should he buy?

20 m
15 m

6 Kate buys a door. The width is stated as 2.64 m (to the nearest centimetre).
She measures the frame as 2.65 m (to the nearest centimetre).
Will the door fit the frame?

7 A 2p coin weighs 7.1 g (to the nearest 0.1 gram).
A machine counts bags of coins by weighing them.
What range of values should it accept for a bag containing £1 in 2p coins?

16.3 Estimating answers

1 Round the numbers in the following calculations to 1 significant figure and find an approximate answer for each one. Then select the correct answer from those given.
   (a) $78.8^2 =$
   (i) 7885.44 **(ii)** 605.284 **(iii)** 6209.44 **(iv)** 605 284
   (b) $\sqrt{384.16} =$
   (i) 19.6 **(ii)** 21.4 **(iii)** 192.08 **(iv)** 14.6
   (c) $(18.76 + 8.9) \times 11.42 =$
   (i) 117.398 **(ii)** 2 816.172 **(iii)** 315.8772 **(iv)** 28 161.72
   (d) $\pi \times 4.3^2 =$ (correct to 3 decimal places)
   (i) 58.088 **(ii)** 16.808 **(iii)** 182.489 **(iv)** 157.914

2 For each part
   (i) make an estimate by rounding each number to 1 significant figure

   (ii) do the calculation on your calculator and write the answer to 3 significant figures.
   (a) $198 \div 21.8$ **(b)** $\pi \times 15.9^2$ **(c)** $\sqrt{9.7^2 - 5.7^2}$
   (d) $22 \times 7.6 \times 19.4$ **(e)** $\dfrac{12.3 + 27.15}{0.098}$ **(f)** $\sqrt{32 \times 51}$
   (g) $703 \div 6.72$ **(h)** $\sqrt[3]{121}$

3 This lorry is transporting a cargo of cans.
The lorry is 2 m wide.
Estimate the number of cans the lorry holds.

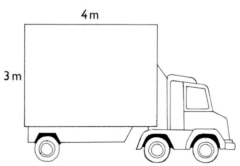

4 m

3 m

11 cm

8 cm

4 Sound travels 330 m in one second. Estimate how many kilometres it travels in one day.

5 Henry drives about 19 miles to work. He makes the journey twice each day, five days a week. He usually works 45 weeks in a year.
Estimate how far he travels to and from work in a year.

6 Helen drives an average of 28 miles a day.
Estimate whether she will reach a total of 6 months or 6000 miles first.

7 A cinema has 47 rows and there are 28 seats in each row. Tickets cost £3.90.
Estimate the total amount of money received when it is full.
Is your estimate an over-estimate or an under-estimate?

17 Three dimensions

17.1 Viewing solids

You will need a ruler and a pair of compasses for this exercise.

1 In each case identify the solid shape.

(a) Plan

Front elevation

Side elevation

(b) Plan

Front elevation

Side elevation

(c) Plan

Front elevation

Side elevation

2 Here are the plan and front elevation of a solid.
Draw the side elevation of the solid.

Front
elevation

Plan

3 A child's toy is made from a solid hemisphere and a cone with the two flat faces joined together.
The base radius of the cone and the hemisphere is 4 cm.
The vertical height of the cone is 5 cm.
Draw an accurate plan and elevation of the toy.

4 The diagram shows a cube of side 4 cm.
Points A, B, C and D are 1 cm away from the corners along the edges on the top face of the cube.
Points I, J, K and L are 1 cm away from the corners along the edges on the bottom face of the cube.
Points E, F, G and H are the midpoints of the vertical edges.

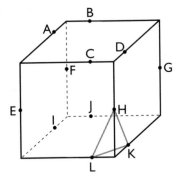

The cube is solid. By slicing through the cube at chosen points you can produce different faces. For example, cutting through the points H, L and K produces a triangular face.

Slicing through which points give the following faces?
(a) A different-sized triangle to HLK
(b) A square
(c) Two different-sized rectangles
(d) A hexagon

17.2 Planes of symmetry

1 The cross-section of this prism is an equilateral triangle.
M, N, O and P, Q, R are the midpoints of the edges of faces ABC and DEF.
AMPD is a plane of symmetry.
(a) Using letters, identify the two other vertical planes of symmetry.
(b) Does this solid have a horizontal plane of symmetry?
(c) The cross-section of another solid is an isosceles triangle.
How many planes of symmetry does the prism have?

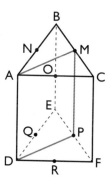

2 ABCD is a regular tetrahedron. M is the midpoint of AB.
MDC is a plane of symmetry.
(a) How many planes of symmetry does the tetrahedron have
in all?
A hexahedron is made by joining two faces of two identical regular
tetrahedra.
(b) How many planes of symmetry does the hexahedron have?

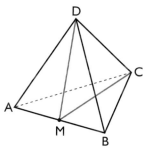

3 In this cube M, N, O, P and Q, R, S, T are the midpoints of
the edges of ABCD and EFGH.
U, V, W and X are the midpoints of the vertical sides.
(a) Using letters, identify the four vertical planes of
symmetry.
(b) How many planes of symmetry does the cube have
altogether? Identify them all.
Hint: A cube has some planes of symmetry which are
neither vertical nor horizontal.

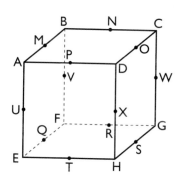

4 These nets of a cube have some of the faces coloured.
(a) How many planes of symmetry does each one have when it is made into a cube?

(i) (ii) 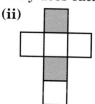 (iii)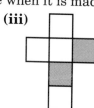

(b) Using only one colour and shading whole faces of the net can you make a net of your
own that has no planes of symmetry when made into a cube?

17.3 Cylinders 🖩

You will need to use the formulae for the volume and the surface area of a cylinder.

Volume of a cylinder, $V = \pi r^2 h$
Total surface area of a cylinder, $S = 2\pi rh$ (walls) $+ \pi r^2$ (top) $+ \pi r^2$ (bottom)

You will need a ruler and a pair of compasses for this exercise.

1 Find the volume and curved surface area of each of these cylinders.

(a)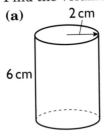

(b)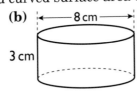

(c)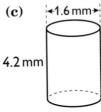

(d)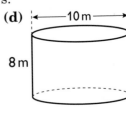

2 A paddling pool is cylindrical with a diameter of 150 cm.
David fills the pool to a depth of 25 cm.
(a) What is the volume of water in the pool in litres?
1 cm³ of water weighs 1 gram.
(b) What is the weight of the water in the pool in kilograms?

3 Rosemary is covering a cylindrical lamp shade with parchment.
The parchment is glued with a 1 cm overlap.
What area of parchment is needed to cover the lampshade?

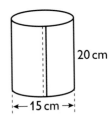

4 Draw an accurate net for a cylinder with radius 3 cm and height 4 cm.

5 A large cylindrical can has a diameter of 10 cm and a height of 20 cm.
(a) The can is full of soup. What volume of soup does it contain?
The soup is poured into some cylindrical mugs.
The mugs have a diameter of 5 cm and a height of 8 cm.
(b) How many mugs can be filled?

6 A cylindrical concrete pipe has an outer diameter of 10 cm. The concrete is 1 cm thick.
What volume of concrete is used to make a pipe of length 75 cm?

7 **Investigation** ───────

In each part the height of the cylinder is the same as the radius.
(a) The number of cm³ in the volume is the same as the
number of cm² in its curved surface area.
What are the radius and volume of the cylinder?
(b) The number of cm³ in the volume is the same as the
number of cm² in its total surface area.
What are the radius and volume of the cylinder?

Tip: Leave the volume and area as multiples of π.

18 Real life graphs

18.1 Shapes of graphs

You will need graph paper for this exercise.

1 The table shows Sandra's pulse rate, in beats per minute, as she exercises.

Time (minutes)	0	1	2	3	4	5	6	7	8	9	10
Pulse rate (bpm)	72	80	100	135	132	125	110	100	95	90	87

(a) Show this information as a smooth curve on a graph.
(b) During which minute does Sandra's pulse rate rise most quickly?
(c) During which minute does her pulse rate fall most quickly?
(d) Estimate for how long her pulse rate exceeds 110 beats per minute.

2 The graph shows the speed of a motorcycle at the start of its journey.

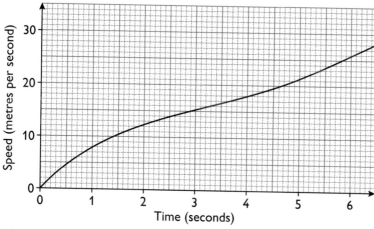

(a) What is the speed of the motorcycle after **(i)** 2 seconds **(ii)** 4.2 seconds?
(b) After how many seconds is the speed **(i)** 12 ms^{-1} **(ii)** 22 ms^{-1}?

3 Samantha keeps a running total of the number of text messages she sends one week. The chart shows this information.

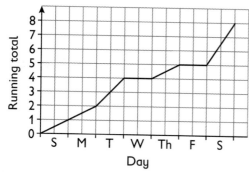

(a) How many text messages does Samantha send in the week?
(b) On which days does she send no text messages?
(c) How many text messages does she send on Saturday?
(d) On which day of the week does she send two text messages?

4   The table shows the water level in a river for one day.

Time after midnight (hours)	0	2	4	6	8	10	12	14	16	18	20	22	24
Water level (metres)	0.85	0.95	1.30	1.55	1.80	2.35	2.50	2.70	2.60	2.35	2.30	2.10	1.85

(a)   Show this information as a smooth curve. Use 1 cm for 1 hour and 4 cm for 1 m.

(b)   Estimate the water level at 7 pm.

(c)   A flood warning is given when the water level reaches 2 m or more.
      At what time is the flood warning given?

5   Water is poured into each of these containers at a constant rate.
Sketch graphs showing how the water level rises with time.

(a) 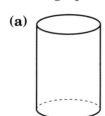   (b) 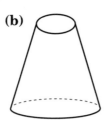   (c) 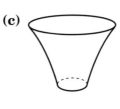   (d)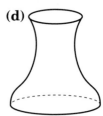

18.2 Working with equations of graphs

You will need graph paper for this exercise.

1 **(a)** Show that the area, A cm^2, of this rectangle is
$A = x^2 - 5x$.
(b) Explain why x must be greater than 5.
(c) Copy and complete this table.

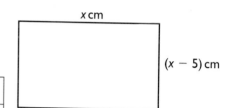

x cm

$(x - 5)$ cm

x	5	6	7	8	9	10
x^2	25					
$-5x$	-25					
$A = x^2 - 5x$	0					

(d) Take x from 5 to 10 and plot a graph of A against x.
(e) Use your graph to estimate the dimensions of the rectangle that has an area of 30 cm^2.

2 In a cricket match a batsman hits the ball so that its flight is given by the equation
$$h = \frac{4x}{3} - \frac{x^2}{45}$$
where h is the height of the ball, in metres, after travelling a horizontal distance of x metres.
(a) Plot a graph of h against x for values of x from 0 to 60.
(b) What is the greatest height of the ball?
(c) Estimate the horizontal distances travelled by the ball when its height is 17 m.
(d) The batsman scores six runs if the ball lands outside the boundary rope?
He scores 6. How far is the boundary rope from the batsman?

3 The formula for the volume, V cm^3, of this cuboid is
$V = x^3 + 4x^2$.
(a) Plot the graph of V against x for values of x from 0 to 4.
(b) Use your graph to estimate the volume of the cuboid
when $x = 3.2$.
(c) Use your graph to estimate the value of x when $V = 90$.

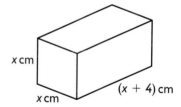

x cm

x cm

$(x + 4)$ cm

4 This right-angled triangle has an area of 150 cm^2.
The length of the base, b cm is given by $b = 35 - h$.
(a) Show that $35h - h^2 = 300$.
(b) Draw a suitable graph and use it to estimate h.
(c) What values of b and h would make the area of the
triangle a maximum?

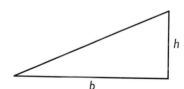

h

b

19 Transformations

19.1 Transformations

You will need squared paper for this exercise.

1 For each diagram describe fully the transformation which maps A to B.

(a)
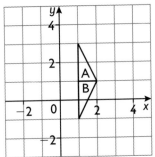

(b)
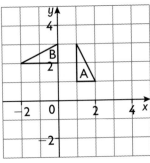

(c)
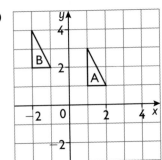

(d)
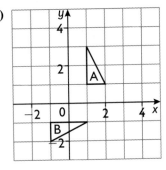

2 (a) (i) Draw and label x and y axes from -6 to 6.
  (ii) Plot the following points and join them to form a parallelogram. Label it P.

$$(1, 1), (4, 1), (5, 2), (2, 2)$$

(b) (i) Rotate P through 90° clockwise about (0, 1). Label the image A.
  (ii) Reflect A in $x = 0$. Label the image B.

(c) (i) Translate P by $\begin{pmatrix} -3 \\ 1 \end{pmatrix}$. Label the image C.

  (ii) Describe the transformation which maps A to C.

3 (a) (i) Draw and label x and y axes from -6 to 6.
  (ii) Plot the following points and join them to form a triangle. Label it T.

$$(1, 0), (2, 0), (2, 2)$$

(b) (i) Rotate T through 180° about (0, 0). Label the image A.
  (ii) Translate A by $\begin{pmatrix} 2 \\ 3 \end{pmatrix}$. Label the image B.

(c) Describe the single transformation which maps T to B.
(d) Draw another diagram showing T.
(e) (i) Translate T by $\begin{pmatrix} 2 \\ 3 \end{pmatrix}$. Label the image D.

  (ii) Rotate D through 180° about (0, 0). Label the image E.
(f) Describe the single transformation which maps T to E.

4   Investigation

(a)   **(i)**   Draw and label x and y axes from -6 to 6.

     (ii)   Plot the following points and join them to form a triangle. Label it T.

$$(2, 0), (3, 0), (2, 2)$$

     (iii) Reflect T in $y = x$. Label the image A.

     (iv) Reflect A in $y = 2$. Label the image B.

     (v)   Describe the single transformation which maps T to B.

(b)   Now test these pairs of transformations in the same way as in **(a)**. In each case state a single transformation which is equivalent to the two transformations.

     (i)   Reflection in $y = x$ and in $x = 2$.

     (ii)   Reflection in $y = x + 1$ and in $y = 3$.

(c)   **(i)**   Make a prediction about the single transformation which is equivalent to reflection in $y = x + 2$ and in $x = 1$.

     (ii)   Test your prediction.

19.2 Enlargement and similar figures

You will need squared paper for this exercise.

1 **(a)** Describe fully the transformation which maps

    (i) A → B   **(ii)** C → D.

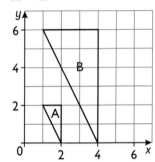 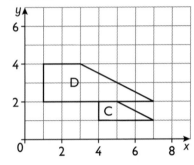

    (b) What is the relationship between the angles of

        (i) triangles A and B   **(ii)** trapezia C and D.

2 Draw and label x and y axes from 0 to 17.

    (a) Draw the trapezium with vertices (4, 2), (6, 2), (7, 4) and (4, 4). Label it ABCD.

    (b) Enlarge ABCD with centre (0, 0) and scale factor 2 to form A′B′C′D′.

    (c) Enlarge ABCD with centre (2, 0) and scale factor 3 to form A″B″C″D″.

    (d) Describe the single transformation which maps A′B′C′D′ to A″B″C″D″.

3 Draw and label x and y axes from 0 to 15.

    (a) Draw the rectangle with vertices (11, 2), (14, 2), (14, 4) and (11, 4). Label it ABCD.

    (b) Enlarge ABCD with centre (15, 1) and scale factor 2 to form A′B′C′D′.

    (c) Enlarge A′B′C′D′ with centre (14, 2) and scale factor 2 to form A″B″C″D″.

    (d) Work out the following ratios.

        (i) Perimeter of ABCD : Perimeter of A′B′C′D′ : Perimeter of A″B″C″D″

        (ii) Area of ABCD : Area of A′B′C′D′ : Area of A″B″C″D″

    (e) Without any further drawing, write down the ratios in **(d)** when **(b)** and **(c)** are repeated using a scale factor of 3.

4 Investigation

Draw and label x and y axes from -3 to 15.

(a) Draw the quadrilateral with vertices (1, 2), (2, 2), (3, 4) and (2, 5). Label it Q.

(b) Enlarge Q with centre (0, 0) and scale factor 3. Label the image A.

Translate A by $\begin{pmatrix} -2 \\ -4 \end{pmatrix}$. Label the image B.

Describe the single transformation which maps Q to B.

(c) Enlarge Q with centre (1, 1) and scale factor 3. Label the image C.

Translate C by $\begin{pmatrix} 0 \\ -4 \end{pmatrix}$. Label the image D.

Describe the single transformation which maps Q to D.

(d) Enlarge Q with centre (1, 0) and scale factor 3. Label the image E.

Translate E by $\begin{pmatrix} 4 \\ 2 \end{pmatrix}$. Label the image F.

Describe the single transformation which maps Q to F.

(e) Predict the single transformation that is the same as an enlargement with centre (0, 3) and scale factor 3 and a translation of $\begin{pmatrix} -2 \\ 4 \end{pmatrix}$. Test your prediction.

(f) State a general rule for the single transformation which replaces an enlargement followed by a translation.

19.3 Fractional enlargements

You will need squared paper for this exercise.

1 **(a)** Describe fully the enlargement which maps
    (i) A → B   **(ii)** C → D.

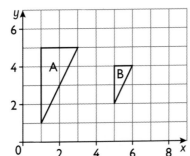 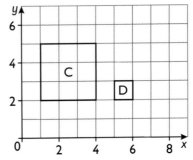

(b) Work out the following ratios.
    (i) side A : side B and area A : area B
    (ii) side C : side D and area C : area D

2 Draw and label x and y axes from 0 to 17.
    (a) Draw the quadrilateral with vertices (10, 16), (12, 12), (12, 8) and (8, 8).
        Label it ABCD.
    (b) Enlarge ABCD with centre (2, 2) and scale factor $\frac{1}{2}$.
        Label the image A′B′C′D′.
    (c) Enlarge ABCD with centre (10, 4) and scale factor $\frac{1}{4}$.
        Label the image A″B″C″D″.
    (d) Describe the single transformation which maps A′B′C′D′ to A″B″C″D″.

3 Kate draws a plan of her lounge. The lounge is 6 m by 4 m.
    On the plan the longer side measures 12 cm.
    (a) **(i)** What is the scale of the plan?
        (ii) On the plan how long is the shorter side?
    (b) A rug in the lounge has an area of 5 m².
        What area does the rug cover on the plan?

④ Investigation

Adam has drawn the net of a cube with side 4 cm.
(a) What is the total surface area of the cube?
(b) What is the volume of the cube?

Adam wants to make an enlargement of the
cube with scale factor $\frac{1}{2}$.
(c) For this copy what is
    (i) the length of the sides
    (ii) the total surface area
    (iii) the volume of the cube?
(d) What enlargement reading does Adam
    need to make a net of a cube with
    (i) half the surface area of the original
        cube
    (ii) half the volume of the original cube?

A photocopier gives a linear scale factor, so I'll set the enlargement reading on the photocopier to 50% to copy my net.

20 Inequalities

20.1 Inequalities

1 Copy the following pairs of values and put the correct inequality sign between them.

(a) 0.6 ☐ 0.5

(b) -0.6 ☐ -0.5

(c) $\frac{1}{3}$ ☐ 0.3

(d) 6p ☐ £0.60

(e) 2 kg ☐ 500 g

(f) -10 ☐ -11

(g) 2^3 ☐ 3^2

(h) 50% ☐ 0.7

(i) $\frac{1}{4}$ ☐ $\frac{1}{5}$

(j) 2 km ☐ 20 000 cm

(k) 0.5 cm ☐ 3 mm

(l) $(-0.5)^2$ ☐ $(-0.6)^2$

2 Write the following statements as inequalities.

(a) A weak bridge has a maximum weight limit of 3.5 tonnes. (Let w stand for the weight in tonnes.)

(b) A football club is going to a tournament and they need at least 8 players with a maximum of 15. (Let p stand for the number of players.)

(c) A jet plane has 400 seats and it is over half full. (Let p stand for the number of passengers on the plane.)

(d) Benley United ground has 44 300 seats. At the last game there were less than 200 empty seats. (Let s stand for the number of spectators at the last game.)

3 For each of the following expressions, list all the possible integer values.

(a) $1 < x < 5$

(b) $-2 \leqslant x < 2$

(c) $0 < x \leqslant 3$

(d) $-1 < x \leqslant 1$

(e) $-5 < x < -3$

(f) $43 \leqslant x \leqslant 47$

(g) $3 < x < 7$

(h) $-2 < x < 2$

(i) $-6 \leqslant x < -1$

(j) $-2 \leqslant x \leqslant 5$

(k) $6 < 2x < 14$

(l) $-5 \leqslant 3x < 7$

20.2   Inequalities on the number line

You may find squared paper useful for this exercise.

1   Write down the inequalities represented by the following number lines.

(a)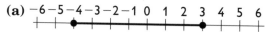

(b)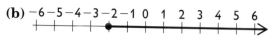

(c) −6 −5 −4 −3 −2 −1 0 1 2 3 4 5 6

(d) −6 −5 −4 −3 −2 −1 0 1 2 3 4 5 6

2   Draw and label number lines from −6 to 6 and show each of these inequalities on a separate number line.

(a) $-2 < x \leqslant 3$ **(b)** $x < 4$ **(c)** $-5 \leqslant x \leqslant -1$

(d) $x < -2$ **(e)** $x \geqslant 0$ **(f)** $0 < x < 4$

3   Solve the following simultaneous inequalities.

(a) $3 \leqslant x \leqslant 15 \; and \; -1 \leqslant x \leqslant 12$

(b) $-5 \leqslant x \leqslant 2 \; and \; -3 \leqslant x \leqslant 4$

(c) $3 \leqslant x \leqslant 9 \; and \; 2 \leqslant x < 6$

(d) $x > -2 \; and \; x < 3$

(e) $-3 < x \leqslant 2 \; and \; -1 < x < 1$

(f) $-4 \leqslant x < 2 \; and \; -6 \leqslant x \leqslant 2$

4   Write the information given in these statements using inequality symbols.

(a)   The house prices on the Holmwood Estate vary between £60 000 and £120 000. Mr and Mrs Gribble live on this estate and their house is worth £v.

(b)   Miss Robinson's classroom has 32 seats. There are b boys and g girls in her class.

(c)   A cinema has a maximum of 240 seats. For one film there are a adults and c children.

(d)   The minimum qualifying time for the Great South Run is 72 minutes. Let t stand for the time, in minutes, taken by a participant.

20.3 Solving inequalities

You will need squared paper for this exercise.

1 Mirna packs magazines into six identical boxes.
  (a) Using w for the weight of each box, write an expression for the combined weight of all the boxes.
  (b) There are a few magazines left over. These weigh 2 kg. Write an expression for the weight of all the magazines.
  (c) Mirna knows that the magazines weigh at least 50 kg. Write this statement as an inequality and solve it.

2 Tim takes himself, two other adults and six children to a cinema.
  A child's ticket costs one pound less than an adult's ticket.
  (a) Using a for the cost of an adult's ticket, write an expression for the cost of all the tickets and simplify it.
  (b) He paid for the tickets and received some change from £30.
    Write an inequality with this information and solve it.

3 Solve these inequalities.
  (a) $5x \geqslant 30$
  (b) $3x + 1 \leqslant 10$
  (c) $2x - 5 > 27$
  (d) $x + 1 < 1$
  (e) $4(x - 3) \geqslant 24$
  (f) $3(2x + 1) < 15$
  (g) $\frac{1}{2}x - 2 \leqslant -3$
  (h) $\frac{1}{3}(x + 2) \geqslant 4$

4 Solve these inequalities.
  (a) $1 - x \leqslant 1$
  (b) $5 - x > 2$
  (c) $3 - 2x < 7$
  (d) $3(2 - x) \geqslant 9$
  (e) $5(1 - 2x) \leqslant 20$
  (f) $5x + 2 < 3x + 4$
  (g) $6(x - 3) \geqslant 2x - 2$
  (h) $1 - 3x < 5x - 3$

5 **(a)** Draw axes taking values of x and y from 0 to 6.
  (b) Draw the lines $x = 3$, $y = 2$ and $x + y = 8$ on your graph.
  (c) Circle the integer points which satisfy these inequalities.

  $x \geqslant 3$ and $y \geqslant 2$ and $x + y \leqslant 8$

6 Draw a graph to show the integer points which satisfy these inequalities.

  $y \geqslant 1$ and $y \leqslant x + 1$ and $x + y \leqslant 5$

21 Probability

21.1 Calculating probabilities

1 A multiple choice question gives five alternatives, only one of which is correct.
Mike guesses one of the choices at random.
What is the probability of him choosing
   (a) the correct answer   **(b)** the wrong answer?

2 A book has 40 pages; there are pictures on 17 of them.
I open the book at random.
What is the probability of opening at a page
   (a) which has a picture   **(b)** which does not have a picture?

3 The diagram shows the seating plan of a small aeroplane.
Elaine is the first passenger to book in. She is given a seat at random.
What is the probability that
   (a) it is a window seat
   (b) it is next to the aisle
   (c) it is both a window seat and next to the aisle
   (d) it is neither a window seat nor next to the aisle
   (e) it is either a window seat or next to the aisle but not both?

3	A	2	1
3	B	2	1
3	C	2	1
3	D	2	1
3	E	2	1

Door   Door

3	2	F	1
3	2	G	1
3	2	H	1
3	2	I	1
3	2	J	1

4 A type of plant has either pink flowers or white flowers in the ratio 1 : 3.
   (a) What is the probability that a plant chosen at random has
      (i) pink flowers   **(ii)** white flowers?
   (b) James picks 300 plants. How many does he expect to have pink flowers?

5 Alice's biscuit tin contains 8 chocolate biscuits and 28 plain biscuits.
   (a) She chooses a biscuit without looking.
      What is the probability that it is a chocolate one?
   (b) The first biscuit was, in fact, a chocolate one. She eats it then chooses another biscuit
      at random. What is the probability that it is also chocolate?

6 Darius' fridge contains ten cans of cola and six cans of lemonade.
   (a) He takes a can from the fridge without looking.
      What is the probability that it is a can of lemonade?
   (b) The first can was, in fact, of lemonade. He drinks it then chooses another can at
      random. What is the probability that it is a can of cola?

7 A new shoe shop buys equal numbers of 60 different styles of ladies' shoes.

Type	Sandals	Boots	High heels	Sling backs	Trainers
Frequency	8	12	13	8	19

(a) An assistant picks up a box of ladies' shoes at random.
What is the probability that it contains
   (i) sandals   (ii) trainers
   (iii) not boots   (iv) either sandals or boots?

(b) There are 1200 boxes of shoes in the store.
How many boxes would you expect to contain
   (i) sling backs   (ii) boots or trainers   (iii) not high heels?

21.2 Combined outcomes

1 (a) Make a list of all the ways in which the three letters T, R and A can be arranged.
(b) The three letters are written down at random. What is the probability that
   (i) they spell TAR
   (ii) they spell a word
   (iii) they will be in alphabetical order?

2 (a) Make a list of all the different three-figure numbers which can be formed using the digits 2, 3 and 5 if none is repeated.
(b) What is the probability of selecting one of these numbers at random and it being
   (i) a number greater than 500
   (ii) a number less than 200
   (iii) an even number
   (iv) a multiple of 25?
(c) How many different three-figure numbers will there be if the digits can be repeated?

3 A delivery firm has five lorries labelled A, B, C, D and E.
Each day the firm uses just three of the lorries while one is serviced and another is cleaned.
(a) Copy and complete the table to show all the different possible pairs of lorries not being used on one day.
(b) Why are some of the sections shaded?
(c) How many possible pairs are there?
(d) What is the probability that on any one day
   (i) one of the lorries not being used is A
   (ii) either A or B is not being used but not both of them
   (iii) lorry E is being used?
(e) On 40 working days, how many times would you expect lorry A to be used?

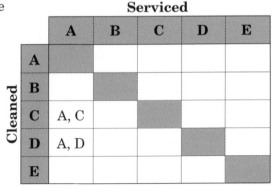

Serviced / Cleaned table:

Cleaned \ Serviced	A	B	C	D	E
A					
B					
C	A, C				
D	A, D				
E					

21.3 Estimating probabilities

You will need squared paper and a pack of playing cards for the activity in this exercise.

1 During one week, a garage sells 30 new cars. A record is kept of the number of visits each car has to make to the garage to have faults put right.

Number of visits	0	1	2	3	4	5	6	7
Number of cars	6	12	5	1	1	2	2	1

(a) What is the probability that a car, chosen at random, is brought back
  (i)   twice   (ii) not at all
  (iii) more than three times   (iv) at least once?

(b) The next week the garage sells 20 cars.
  Estimate the number of cars they expect to be brought back
  (i)   not at all   (ii) more than three times.

2 Terry noted the different species of bird that landed in his garden.
The bar chart shows the results for the first 100 birds.

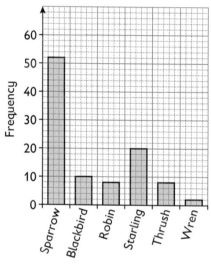

(a) What is the probability that the next bird to land in the garden is
  (i)   a robin
  (ii) a blackbird
  (iii) a starling or a sparrow
  (iv) not a wren
  (v)   not a thrush?

(b) The following day, Terry sees 25 birds in his garden.
  Estimate the number of
  (i)   starlings
  (ii) thrushes.

3 **Activity**

(a) What is the probability of cutting a normal pack of 52 playing cards and getting a diamond? Write your answer as a decimal.

(b) Take a pack of playing cards.

   (i) Copy this table.

Number of cuts of the pack	10	20	30	40	50	60
Number of diamonds						
Experimental probability						

   (ii) Cut the pack ten times and record the number of times the card is a diamond. Write your experimental probability as a decimal.

   (iii) Cut the pack a further 10 times, making 20 times in all. Fill in the table for 20 cuts.

   (iv) Continue cutting the pack until you have completed the table.

   (v) Copy these axes. Draw a graph of the experimental probabilities.

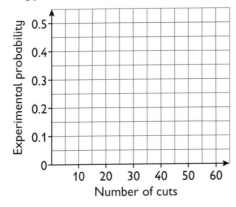

(c) What do you notice?

(d) What would happen if you increased the number of cuts to 1000?

Trigonometry

22.1 Right-angled triangles

1 Sketch each of these right-angled triangles.
Label the hypotenuse, opposite and adjacent sides using H, O and A.

(a) **(b)** **(c)** **(d)**

(e) **(f)** **(g)** 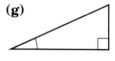 **(h)**

2 For each of these triangles
   (i) use Pythagoras' theorem to show that it is right-angled
   (ii) work out the three ratios, $\dfrac{O}{H}$, $\dfrac{A}{H}$ and $\dfrac{O}{A}$.

Which of the triangles are similar to each other?

(a) **(b)** 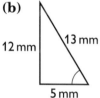 **(c)** 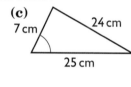 **(d)**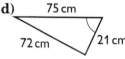

(e) 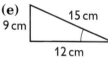 **(f)** 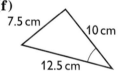 **(g)** 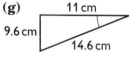 **(h)**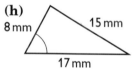

(i) **(j)** 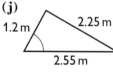 **(k)** 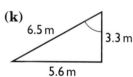 **(l)**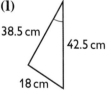

3 For each of these triangles
   (i) use Pythagoras' theorem to work out the missing side
   (ii) find the three ratios, $\dfrac{O}{H}$, $\dfrac{A}{H}$ and $\dfrac{O}{A}$.

Which of the triangles are similar to each other?

(a) 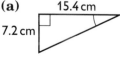 **(b)** **(c)** 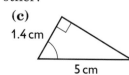 **(d)**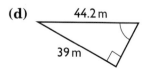

22.2 Trigonometrical ratios

1 (a) Draw a horizontal line of any length.
  (b) Draw an angle of 35° from the left-hand end and make a right-angled triangle.
  (c) Measure H, O and A.
  (d) Use your measurements to work out sin 35°, cos 35° and tan 35°.

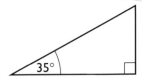

2 For each of these triangles, write down
  (i) the names (using H, O or A) of the two sides which are given
  (ii) the name and value of the trigonometrical ratio that involves these two sides.

(a)   (b) 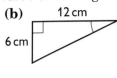 (c) 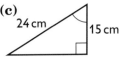 (d)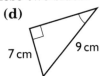

(e) 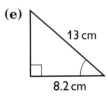 (f) 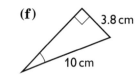 (g) 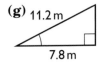 (h)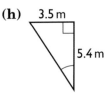

3 For each of these triangles, work out the value of sin θ, cos θ and tan θ.

(a) 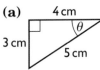 (b) 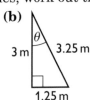 (c) 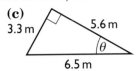 (d)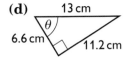

(e) 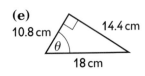 (f) 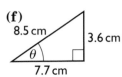 (g) 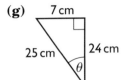 (h)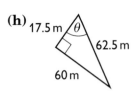

4 For each of these triangles
  (i) use Pythagoras' theorem to work out the missing side
  (ii) find the value of the three trig. ratios, sin θ, cos θ and tan θ.

(a) (b) 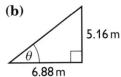 (c) 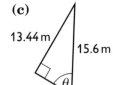 (d)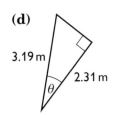

22.3 Finding lengths

In this exercise give your answer to 2 decimal places where necessary.

1   For each of these triangles, find the length labelled x.

(a)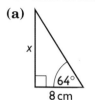

(b)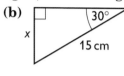

(c)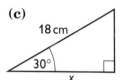

(d)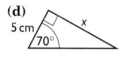

(e)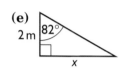

(f)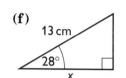

(g)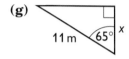

(h)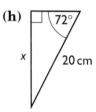

2   For each of these triangles, find the lengths labelled x and y.

(a)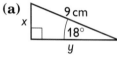

(b)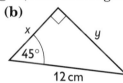

(c)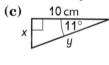

(d)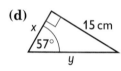

(e)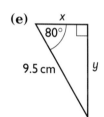

(f)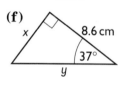

(g)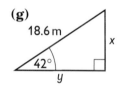

(h)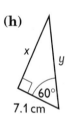

(i)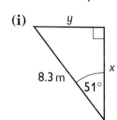

(j)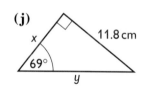

(k)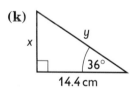

(l)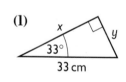

3   A ladder 2.9 m long rests against a wall and makes an angle of 70° with the horizontal.
  (a)   How high up the wall does the ladder reach?
  (b)   How far from the bottom of the wall is the foot of the ladder?

4   The diagonal of a rectangle is 12.5 cm long and makes an angle of 40° with the longer side.
  (a)   Calculate the length of the longer side.
  (b)   Calculate the length of the shorter side.

5   A helicopter flies 50 km from its base on a bearing 125°.
  How far south and how far east does it travel?

22.4 Finding angles

In this exercise give your answer to 2 decimal places where necessary.

1 Use your calculator to find θ.
(a) $\sin \theta = 0.766$ (b) $\cos \theta = 0.766$ (c) $\tan \theta = 0.577$ (d) $\sin \theta = 0.309$
(e) $\cos \theta = 0.309$ (f) $\tan \theta = 1.4$ (g) $\tan \theta = 2.05$ (h) $\sin \theta = 0.99$
(i) $\cos \theta = 0.99$ (j) $\cos \theta = 0.245$ (k) $\tan \theta = 1.834$ (l) $\sin \theta = 0.665$
(m) $\tan \theta = 0.333$ (n) $\cos \theta = 0.496$ (o) $\tan \theta = 0.417$ (p) $\sin \theta = 0.702$

2 Find angle θ in each of these triangles.

(a) 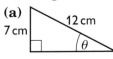   (b) 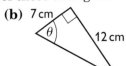   (c) 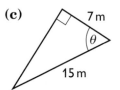   (d)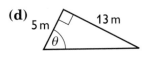

(e)   (f) 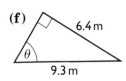   (g) 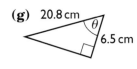   (h)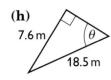

(i)    (j) 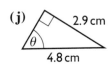   (k) 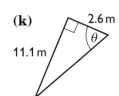   (l)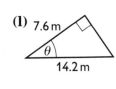

3 A wheelbarrow ramp is 6.1 m long. One end rests on horizontal ground and the other rests on the edge of a rubbish skip. The top of the ramp is 1.8 m above its lower end. What angle does the ramp make with the horizontal?

4 A boat sails 45 km north from P to Q.
It then sails 60 km east from Q to R.
(a) Draw a sketch showing P, Q and R.
(b) Calculate the bearing of R from P.
(c) Calculate the distance from P to R.
(d) What is the bearing of P from R?

5 A cable is set up from the top of a building.
The building is 50 m high and the cable is anchored 76 m away from the building.
What angle does the cable make with the ground?

6 The diagram shows the cross-section of a roof.
(a) Calculate the height, AD, of the roof.
(b) Calculate the length DC.
(c) Calculate the angle AC makes with the horizontal.

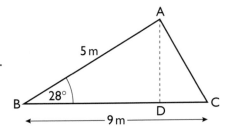

23 Reasoning

23.1 Proof

1 Find a counter-example for each of these conjectures.
   (a) The product of two numbers is greater than both numbers.
   (b) Division makes a number smaller.
   (c) Shapes that have rotation symmetry also have reflection symmetry.
   (d) The last digit in a prime number is itself prime.

2 Goldbach's Conjecture states that 'You can split every even number from 4 onwards into the sum of two prime numbers'. It has never been proved.
Here is a similar conjecture.

   Any number, apart from 1, is either prime or is the sum of two primes.

Disprove it by finding a counter-example.

3 Prove this conjecture using proof by exhaustion.

   Using only 2s and 3s it is possible to make additions with answers equal to all the whole numbers from 4 to 11. For example: $7 = 2 + 2 + 3$.

4 Disprove this conjecture by finding a counter-example.

   No triangular number is also a square number.

5 Prove that it is impossible to construct a 2 by 2 magic square.

6 Disprove this conjecture by finding a counter-example.

   The number of different n-letter 'words' made by arranging n different letters is $2n$.

For example when $n = 3$, using say, the letters A, B and C the 'words' are

   ABC   ACB   BAC   BCA   CAB   CBA.

7 Bethany has a large supply of 1p, 2p and 3p stamps.
She uses the stamps to make different totals.
For example, there are four ways she can make a total of 4p.

This table shows the number of different ways various totals can be made.

Total (p)	1	2	3	4
Number of ways	1	2	3	4

Bethany makes the conjecture that there are n different ways to make a total n pence using 1p, 2p and 3p stamps.
Disprove Bethany's conjecture by finding a counter-example.

23.2 Using algebra for proof

1 Here are some expressions involving n, where n is a positive whole number.
   (i) $2n$ **(ii)** $3n + 6$ **(iii)** $2n + 1$ **(iv)** $4n + 1$ **(v)** $4n + 4$
Which expression(s) give numbers which are always
   (a) odd   **(b)** even   **(c)** divisible by 3   **(d)** divisible by 4?

2 Write any four numbers at the corners of a square.

Add the numbers at the ends of each side.
Write the answers on the sides.

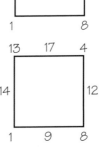

Add the four corner numbers.

$$1 + 13 + 4 + 8 = 26$$

Add the four side numbers.

$$14 + 17 + 12 + 9 = 52$$
$$\text{which is } 2 \times 26$$

Prove, using letters, that the sum of the side numbers is always twice the sum of the corner numbers.

3 A sequence in which each term is the sum of the two previous terms is called a Fibonacci-type sequence.
Beneta looked at this Fibonacci-type sequence.

     2, 5, 7, 12, 19, 31, 50, …

She noticed
   (i)   that the first and fourth term added together were equal to twice the third term
   (ii) that the sum of the first six terms, which is 76, is equal to four times the fifth term
       ($4 \times 19 = 76$)
   (iii) that the sum of the first 10 terms was equal to 11 times the seventh term.

She found the same was true for the sequence 1, 1, 2, 3, 5, ….
   (a) Let a and b be the first two terms of a Fibonacci-type sequence.
       Write down the first 12 terms.
   (b) Show that Beneta's three findings are true for any Fibonacci-type sequence.

4 Here is part of a hundred square.

1	2	3	4	5	6	7	8	9	10
11	12	13	14	15	16	17	18	19	20
21	22	23	24	25	26	27	28	29	30
31	32	33	34	35	36	37	38	39	40
41	42	43	44	45	46	47	48	49	50

Here is a 3 by 3 section of a hundred square.

14	15	16
24	25	26
34	35	36

(a) The sum of the top left number and the bottom right number, $14 + 36 = 50$, is equal to the sum of the top right number and the bottom left number, $16 + 34 = 50$.

(b) Both sums in **(a)** are equal to 22 more than twice the top left number, $22 + 2 \times 14 = 22 + 28 = 50$.

Prove that these results are always true.

Hint: Let the top left number be x, the next number be $x + 1$ and so on.

23.3 Proof in geometry: angles

You will need to use these angle facts to answer the questions in this exercise.
① Angles on a straight line sum to 180°.
② Angles round a point sum to 360°.
③ Alternate angles are equal.
④ Corresponding angles are equal.
⑤ Vertically opposite angles are equal.

1 **(a)** Complete this proof that vertically opposite angles are equal. It only uses fact ①.
The straight lines AB and CD intersect at O.
Let $A\hat{O}C = R°$
$A\hat{O}C + A\hat{O}D = 180°$ (_____)
So $A\hat{O}D = 180° - R°$
But $C\hat{O}B$ is also $= 180° - R°$ (_____)
Therefore $A\hat{O}D = C\hat{O}B$

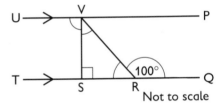

(b) Write a similar proof to show that $A\hat{O}C = D\hat{O}B$.

2 *PU* and *QT* are parallel. $Q\hat{R}V = 100°$ and $V\hat{S}R = 90°$.
Use angle facts to prove that
(a) $V\hat{R}S = 80°$
(b) $S\hat{V}R = 10°$
(c) $S\hat{V}U = 90°$.

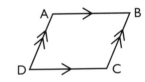

3 Use one or more of the angle facts at the top of the page to prove
that the opposite angles in a parallelogram are equal.
Hint: You will find drawing a diagonal useful.

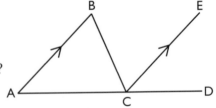

4 **(a)** Use angle facts and this diagram to prove that the
sum of the interior angles of a triangle is 180°.
(b) How can you use the result in **(a)** to show that the
sum of the interior angles of a quadrilateral is 360°?

5 Look at this diagram.
Prove that $A\hat{B}E = 60°$.
Give your reasoning at each step.

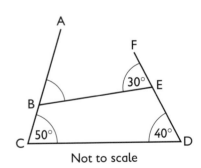

Not to scale

23.4 Proof in geometry: circles

In this exercise the centre of the circle is labelled O.

1 ABCD is a quadrilateral inscribed in a circle.
AC is a diameter of the circle.
Prove that
(a) $A\hat{B}O = 55°$
(b) $A\hat{D}O = 70°$.

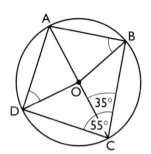

2 *ROT* is a straight line.
The reflex angle $T\hat{O}S = 260°$.
Prove that
(a) $O\hat{T}S = 40°$
(b) $S\hat{O}R = 80°$.

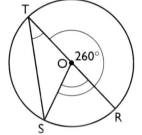

3 MN is a diameter of the circle.
MQ and NP are parallel.
(a) Find
    (i) $Q\hat{O}M$
    (ii) $Q\hat{O}N$
    (iii) x
    (iv) y.
Give your reasoning at each step.
(b) Prove that $M\hat{Q}N = 90°$.

4 ABC is an equilateral triangle inscribed inside a circle.

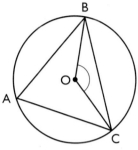

Prove that $B\hat{O}C = 120°$.

5 Prove that $P\hat{O}R = 2 \times (O\hat{P}Q + O\hat{R}Q)$.

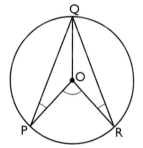

6 **Investigation** ────────────────

Experiment with the geometry program on the site
www.members.shaw.ca/ron.blond/Circle.Geom1.APPLET/index.html
It will help you revise some of the angle facts.

23.5 Logic

1 Twenty people are sitting round a table. A prize of £10 000 is to be divided amongst them so that each person gets half the sum of money that their two neighbours get.
Find a way of sharing the money.
Is there more than one way?

2 There are five children in a family.
On Monday, four go swimming. The total of their ages is 38.
On Tuesday night, four go to a rock concert. The total of their ages is 35.
On Wednesday, four go to a disco. The total of their ages is 36.
On Thursday, four go rollerskating. Their total age is also 36.
Four go shopping on Friday. The total of their ages is 38.
Finally on Saturday, four go to a football match. Their total age is 39.
No person goes out on all six days. What are the ages of the children?

3 A lorry can carry up to 2 tonnes.
The following loads need to be delivered to a building site.

Load	A	B	C	D	E	F	G	H	I	J
Weight (*t*)	1.7	1.2	0.8	1.5	0.4	0.7	0.1	1.8	0.3	1.5

What is the smallest number of journeys which will be needed to deliver all the loads?
(Hint: Think of systematically filling up lorries with the loads.)

4 Here are six crates of machine parts.
Each crate contains bolts, rods or nuts.
There are twice the weight of bolts as rods.
Only one crate contains nuts.
Work out what each crate contains.

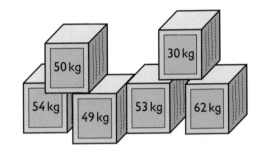

5 Three students Amber, Barry and Caitlin have just received their exam results for maths, English and history. Each student makes two truthful statements.

Amber: My maths result was the same as Barry's.
My English result was the same as Caitlin's.
Barry: If I passed English then so did Amber.
Amber did not pass history.
Caitlin: Either Amber passed history or I did not pass it.
Both the others passed more subjects than me.

All the students passed at least one subject and each subject was passed by at least one student. Which subjects did each of the students pass?